www.jennstoker.com

Requests for permission to make copies of any
part of the work should be submitted online
to info@mascotbooks.com or mailed to:

Mascot Books
560 Herndon Parkway #120
Herndon, VA 20170.

ISBN-10: 1-620860-61-9
ISBN-13: 978-1-620860-61-8
CPSIA Code: PRT0213A

Cover artwork by Danny Moore

Printed in the United States of America

www.mascotbooks.com

She Cooks, She Scores

THE STEAMY STORIES BEHIND THE RECIPES

BY JENNIFER F. STOKER

PHOTOGRAPHY BY EDDIE ENG

About

Chef Jenn

Jenn Stoker obtained her Bachelor of Science from the University of Kansas. She pursued her degree and worked in the film and television arena for six years. Simultaneously, she embarked on an acting career, appearing in commercials and independent films, hosting several talk shows, and working in sports television. The culinary vision came to her when she sold her very own salsa at a farmers' market in Kansas City. The one person she can thank for putting the idea in her head to go to culinary school is her Aunt Carolyn. After a year of summoning up the courage to do it, Jenn packed up a U-Haul and drove from Kansas City to Hyde Park, New York, to attend the Culinary Institute of America (CIA). She had no prior cooking experience, yet she enrolled in the most challenging and prestigious culinary school in the world. During her time at the institute, she did an apprenticeship at Food Network and worked with some of the hottest celebrity chefs. After two grueling years of chef training, she earned a culinary degree and a fellowship to join the staff of one of the restaurants on the CIA campus. Things started to fall into place after she graduated. She was offered a great position with a food service company and started her own business as a personal chef. Intertwined with all of that, she was asked to costar in a fourteen-episode pilot cooking show and host a CIA DVD series. She also conducted a myriad of chef demonstrations throughout the United States, landed a few culinary commercials, worked on this book, and moved to the best city in America: Chicago.

As far as I've come, my life has been one exhilarating, roller-coaster experience after another. I always look at my life and think that I'm the luckiest person because I'm living the dream. Courage and doing the unthinkable has brought me to where I am today. All of my training, hard work, dedication, and everything I have done in my life have come down to this one moment. I am ready to let the world see what I'm all about. Enjoy reading about my wild and crazy adventures.

—Jennifer F. Stoker

Thank You

to all my close friends who stuck by me throughout this whole process and put up with my crazy antics. You are my true friends and I am grateful to have you all in my life.

A big # Thank You to my parents.

I couldn't have done this without you. Your love and support has made me the person I am today. Thank you from the bottom of my heart. I love you both.

Thank You

to the following: Eddie Eng, Uncle T, Scott Stoker, Carolina Toffanelli, ABT appliances, Mark Misicki, Alisa Ireland, Stacy Feldman, Liz Padlo, John Vossoughi, Steve Miksta, Carolina Ordonez, Ron Dulin, Jackie Kim, Shelly Satizabal, Joanna Kuzba, Carolyn Carter, Gail Barnett, Joseph Sultani, Rachael Baird, Enid Seymore, Nick Coveliers, Josh Shoafstall, Susan Murphy, John Wiley, Anthony Scinto, Marc Verdiel, Melissa Rizzo, Holly Hart; CIA instructors Christina Ayala, Gennaro Scopo, Ryan Kellerman, Murali Krishnan, Joe Cinelli, Kim Brown, Avalon team, Cole Kopacek, Charlie Wood, Chelsea Stuck, Annette Ricci, Tom Hopkins, Heather Jordan, and David Chechik.

Table of Contents

ANATOMY OF CHEF JENN

RUNNING

JENN'S PERFECT GUY

FUEL FOR THE FIRE

MAGICAL COMPONENTS FOR JENN'S CREATIONS

marathon
1481

Introduction

MY FIRST FOOD MEMORIES WERE OF COOKING WITH MY GRANDMOTHER AND ALL THE WONDERFUL ITALIAN DISHES THAT SHE CREATED. I WATCHED HER HAND-ROLL PASTA AND SIMMER SAUCES FOR HOURS ON THE STOVE. WATCHING HER PUT CARE AND ATTENTION INTO EVERY DISH AMAZED ME. AFTER THAT, MY AFFECTION FOR FOOD AND COOKING WAS DESTINED TO GROW INTO A LIFELONG LOVE.

In the early eighties, Food Network was nonexistent. Julia Child ran the airwaves and was creating a culinary dynasty. I was nine years old and my childhood friend Becca and I got together every week to watch our favorite TV show line-up: *The Smurfs*, *Strawberry Shortcake*, and Julia Child. I remember being absolutely fascinated by

Julia and her cooking. After her shows, Becca and I would go into the kitchen and get it ready for our cooking show. We cleared off the counters to create a huge space and set up the ingredients. Just as they do on the set of a cooking show, we prepared our ingredients with great care. With my mother pretending she was the camera person, we would perform in front of our imaginary audience. I would go through the dialogue and motions of a poised celebrity chef.

This experience was one of the most significant of my childhood. Little did I know, I was laying the foundation for my future.

I remember when I was eleven years old, my mother took Becca and I to a very upscale French bakery in St. Louis. As soon as we walked in, I noticed the overwhelming, wonderful smell of sweet, buttery pastries, baked bread, and chocolate chip cookies right out of the oven. The glass case was with filled with beautiful, sugary pastries and cookies that I had never seen before. They looked like works of art. The sophistication of the place made me feel like royalty. That culinary experience was so powerful that every time I walk into a bakery or pastry shop, I am instantly brought back to that moment in my childhood.

Everyone can conjure childhood memories that revolve around food. Food, in every culture, is so much more than just something to eat. It's about tradition, experiences, and memories of the people and places we love.

Food is the heart and nucleus of life. It is the epicenter that encompasses us all. Whenever there is a gathering in someone's home, where does everyone congregate? The kitchen, right? Somehow everyone ends up staying in the kitchen because this is where the pulse is generated. Everyone feels some sort of connection to food. The inviting warmth of the kitchen makes this connection come full circle and brings us all together.

With food and beverages we create that comfort zone among friends and family that brings new memories into our lives. Sharing your creations with your loved ones will open a treasure trove of lifelong memories. When I think about the importance of food and people, I get a sense of a special bonding between the two. Not only does food nourish and help us survive on a day-to-day basis, it bridges the gap between us all.

I want to share with you my culinary journey and how all of the recipes in this book came about. Each one has a story behind it. As I said before, family and friends go hand-in-hand with food. This is what connects us and creates significant memories for years to come. The memories created around these recipes mean a lot to me and have changed my life in many ways. I want you to see, taste, and smell the love behind all these dishes and understand what they mean. Without all of the people who came in and out of my life, these recipes and this book would not have been created.

In my opinion, the sauce makes a meal, and without it you have a dull, tasteless dish. I compare all my family and friends to a fine, flavorful sauce—without them, my dishes would be nothing. The sauce is built on layers of flavors and as you create it, the flavors are added in stages. Each flavor component represents a significant part of the recipe. With the right amount of each ingredient, the layers of flavor blend together and a memorable sauce is created. They don't call me the Sauce Queen for nothing.

I dedicate this book to all my family and true friends who have supported me throughout my life. I could not have done this without you all. Thank you. You all are my sauce.

Chapter 1

The Life-Altering Recipes

These recipes were created with the help and inspiration of my family and friends. I started collecting them when I was very young and they have given me long-lasting memories. The recipes in this section were either taught to me or I created them from the inspiration of my loved ones. They were the small steps that made a difference in my life and carried me through this journey. Little did I know that they were leading me to where I am today. There are no coincidences in life and these powerful, small bites prove that theory. It's the little things in life that we take for granted, but we always have to remember that the little stuff makes a huge difference in the end.

Don't be afraid to give your best to what seemingly are small jobs. Every time you conquer one, it makes you that much stronger. If you do the little jobs well, the big ones will tend to take care of themselves.

—Dale Carnegie

Chef Stoker's must-have bites in your kitchen—the staple cooking ingredients

It's the little things in life that make a huge impact. These are my foundation ingredients that all cooks should have in their kitchens. These little ingredients make a huge impact in every dish you will make from this book and in any of your other concoctions.

Must-haves in your kitchen: Vinegar, garlic, onions, chicken stock, canned tomatoes, tomato paste, assorted spices, lemons, Parmesan cheese, pasta, rice, chicken, olive oil, canned beans, bacon, and frozen veggies.

EMMA'S TOMATO SAUCE

I remember this as if it were yesterday. I was eight years old and my grandmother and grandfather had flown into St. Louis to stay with my brother and I while my parents were away. My grandmother was a true Italian cook and she meant business in the kitchen. She spent hours cooking up a storm and I took it all in. Even though I was young, her cooking techniques and how she moved in the kitchen fascinated me. It was like a choreographed dance as she glided with grace and precision.

The most fascinating part was that she didn't use any written recipes; they were all in her head. The way she shaped the raviolis with her ancient-looking pasta tools, rolling the floury gnocchi with a small fork, the fragrant ingredients she added to her tomato sauce, and her crispy city chicken recipe—everything tasted as if she were the head chef at a high-end Italian restaurant.

Being so small, I had to stand on my mother's 70s, paisley, blue and green metal chair to reach the counter. My grandmother and I would roll the gnocchi dough into ropes, cut them into bite-sized pieces, and make the signature fork marks on each and every one of them. I was covered from head to toe in flour. Grandma Emma would make gallons of her homemade tomato sauce and freeze it in containers for my mom. The wonderful smell of her sauce would linger for days in our house. I knew she had a gift for cooking; she was born with the God-given talent and mysteriously that trait was passed on to me.

Grandma Emma's life was cut short when I was in high school. Her sudden death left our family heartbroken. My grandfather, Stanley, came to St. Louis a few months after losing the love of his life. My parents were leaving for a long getaway weekend and it was just my grandfather and I. To cheer his aching heart, I decided to make an Italian meal for him. I had never really cooked a meal before; my mother did all the cooking. So I decided to make a simple tomato sauce and some pasta. I started the tomato sauce from scratch, without any recipes. I knew from watching my grandmother what ingredients went together and what spices tasted good in pasta sauce. My grandfather raved about my pasta and homemade sauce. I think I saw a little smile on his face that night. He said to me, "You already cook like a pro; you had the best teacher." These recipes are dedicated to Grandmother Emma. She would be so proud.

Note: Grandma Emma always told me, when you cook with ground veal and/or pork in any tomato sauce, always add a pinch of cinnamon. It will bring intrigue to your guests' palates.

emma's tomato sauce

EMMA'S TOMATO SAUCE

YIELD: 4 SERVINGS

2 tablespoons olive oil

½ yellow onion, chopped

1 teaspoon fresh garlic, chopped

½ teaspoon dry fennel seeds

1 teaspoon dried oregano

1 tablespoon dried parsley

2 medium-sized tomatoes, chopped

2 (28 oz.) cans whole peeled tomatoes

¼ cup tomato paste

⅓ cup red wine

½ teaspoon sugar

¼ cup fresh basil leaves, chopped

1 tablespoon Parmesan cheese

In large sauce pan, heat olive oil on high. Add onions, garlic, and fennel seeds. Lower heat to medium-high. Cook until onions are translucent and soft. Add oregano and parsley. Mix together. In separate bowl, add whole peeled tomatoes and crush by hand until tomatoes are chunky. To saucepan, add tomatoes, tomato paste, wine, sugar, chopped basil, and Parmesan cheese. Mix together and season to taste with salt and pepper. Let simmer on low heat for 45 minutes. Serve with your favorite pasta.

SCORE TIP:

EMMA'S TOMATO SAUCE

Using canned, whole, peeled tomatoes really brings out the flavor of the tomato in this recipe. By using the whole tomato and not stewed tomatoes that have undergone further processing, you really taste the tomato in its purest form. If you use canned stewed tomatoes, you will not get that nice, robust flavor that the whole tomato possesses. Stewed tomatoes are fine in any recipe that calls for them, but in this recipe you want to achieve that great tomato flavor, and by using canned, whole, peeled tomatoes, you can do that.

If you have tomatoes that are getting soft and mushy, chances are they're about to kick the bucket. Don't throw your money away; save them. Take your dying, non-moldy tomatoes and quarter them. Put in a saucepan on medium-high heat and sprinkle with salt. Let the tomatoes cook down for 30 minutes. Take off heat and allow to cool completely. Put in a plastic, sealable container and freeze for up to two months.

HERBS: This recipe calls for dried herbs because that is what my grandmother Emma used in the original recipe. If you have a wild hair and would like to use fresh herbs in this sauce, here are the measurements that will give you that same amazing flavor:

1 tablespoon fresh chopped parsley
to 2 tablespoons dried parsley flakes

1 teaspoon fresh chopped oregano
to 1 teaspoon dried oregano

bolognese tomato sauce

BOLOGNESE TOMATO SAUCE

YIELD: 4 – 6 SERVINGS

2 tablespoons olive oil

2 teaspoons fresh garlic, chopped fine

1 small yellow onion, diced small

1 lb. ground veal

1 lb. ground pork

2 (28 oz.) cans of whole peeled tomatoes, crush and break apart by hand

3 medium tomatoes, chopped

½ cup good red wine

1 tablespoon balsamic vinegar

⅓ cup fresh basil leaves, chopped

½ teaspoon sugar

1 tablespoon fresh parsley, finely chopped

⅛ teaspoon cinnamon

salt and pepper to taste

In medium stockpot, heat olive oil on high. Add garlic and onions. Reduce heat to medium-high. Cook until onions are translucent and soft, about 7–10 minutes. Add veal and pork. Cook for 10–12 minutes until both meats are thoroughly cooked. Add tomatoes, wine, balsamic, basil, sugar, parsley, and cinnamon. Mix together. Simmer on medium for 45 minutes. With a stick blender or regular blender, puree until sauce is smooth. Add salt and pepper to taste. Blend together and serve over pasta of your choice.

SCORE TIP:

BOLOGNESE

If ground pork or veal does not tickle your fancy in this dish, you can replace it with very lean ground beef, ground turkey, and/or ground chicken, for a lower fat alternative. These will not only still produce the rich, hardy flavor of meaty bolognese, but will be lower in fat and calories. Adding cinnamon to these meat alternatives as well will bring the same full richness to the bolognese sauce. Sauce can be kept in the freezer for up to two months in clean plastic containers with a sealed lid.

Tuscan White Bean and Kale Soup with Hot Sausage

During my first few years at college, I always came home for Thanksgiving and Christmas. On these visits I made soup for everyone. My recipes became so popular among my family and friends that my mom always incorporated them into the holiday menu. She would call me a few days before I came home to ask me what ingredients I needed. This was really my earliest interest in cooking, and I started to realize how food and memories can bring people together.

SCORE TIP:

SOUPS

Making your own stock: Never throw away any bones, vegetable scraps, or shellfish shells. People always make the mistake of throwing these important ingredients out. In these tough economic times, keeping them could really help you save a few bucks and make your dishes taste out of this world. Vegetable scraps you can save include carrot ends, onions parts (wrapper and all), green onion ends, mushroom stems, red pepper tops and ends, leek tops, celery tops and ends, tomato scraps, herb stems, and the list goes on and on.

Leftover turkey and chicken bones, beef bones, and seafood shells can be used instead of throwing them in the garbage. The leftover meat on the bones can add a world of flavor to your stocks. The best thing to use for a chicken stock is a leftover, whole, cooked rotisserie chicken.

Now I know you're saying, "Chef Jenn, how do I have the time to do this?" Well, it's very simple to throw all these scraps into a pot, fill it with water, add salt and a few spices, and let your stovetop do the rest. After 45 minutes on the stove at a medium boil, strain and put into a container to cool. Once cooled, put in your freezer for up to two months. Voilà! See, that wasn't so bad. (See lobster stock recipe for further instructions.)

TUSCAN WHITE BEAN AND KALE SOUP

SCORE TIP:

SUBSTITUTES: If you can't find kale in your grocery store, you can use fresh spinach instead. The spinach will be thinner in consistency than the kale but will achieve that same great taste overall.

Don't want to use Italian sausage and want a flavorful alternative? Replace it with turkey or chicken sausage. Your local grocery store should have a wide variety of sausage flavors to choose from.

Only have dried rosemary in your spice cabinet? Use 2 teaspoons of dried whole rosemary in place of the fresh chopped rosemary.

CUTTING TIP: When cutting your sausage into circles for this recipe, make sure the sausage is slightly frozen. This will help hold the shape and make it easier to cut into circles. If your sausage is not partially frozen, place in freezer for 30–45 minutes until slightly firm.

tomato-basil bisque soup with goat cheese croutons

SCORE TIP:
TOMATO-BASIL BISQUE SOUP

If you are watching your fat and calories, replace the heavy cream with reduced fat or fat free half and half. If you want to turn this into a vegan/nondairy option, use ½ cup softened vegan cream cheese. To soften, put the vegan cream cheese in the microwave for 15–20 seconds, then stir into soup.

TUSCAN WHITE BEAN AND KALE SOUP WITH HOT SAUSAGE

YIELD: 4 – 6 SERVINGS

2 tablespoons olive oil

1 teaspoon fresh garlic, chopped

1 small white onion, chopped

1 tablespoon whole fennel seed

¼ teaspoon red pepper flakes

½ teaspoon garlic salt

1 lb. hot Italian sausage or chicken sausage sliced into ¼-inch circles (for less heat, use sweet Italian sausage)

2 quarts chicken stock

2 medium zucchinis, diced small

2 cups carrots, diced small

2 cans white beans, drained

½ cup tomato puree

½ cup white wine

1 cup water

1 tablespoon apple cider vinegar

4-5 cups kale, chopped into bite-sized pieces

1 teaspoon fresh rosemary, chopped

2 bay leaves

salt and pepper

In medium stockpot, heat olive oil on high. Add garlic, onion, fennel seed, red pepper flakes, and garlic salt. Turn heat down to medium and sauté for 3–4 minutes. Do not burn garlic. Add sausage. Cook for 10–12 minutes until sausage is thoroughly cooked. Add zucchini, carrots, and white beans to pot. Cook for 4–6 minutes. Add tomato puree, wine, water, and chicken stock. Incorporate all ingredients. Bring to boil and then reduce to a simmer. Add kale, rosemary, and bay leaves. Cook for 45 minutes to one hour. Season to taste with salt and pepper. Serve with your favorite crusty bread.

TOMATO-BASIL BISQUE SOUP WITH GOAT CHEESE CROUTONS

YIELD: 4 SERVINGS

2 tablespoons olive oil

1 small red onion, diced small

¼ cup green onions, chopped

1 teaspoon garlic, chopped

1 tablespoon balsamic vinegar

6 vine-ripened tomatoes, chopped

2 (28 oz) cans whole plum tomatoes, crushed by hand

2 ½-3 cups chicken stock

½ cup red wine

¾ cup basil leaves, torn

1 tablespoon fresh parsley, chopped

¼ teaspoon red pepper flakes

⅓ cup Parmesan cheese

salt and pepper

large round croutons or French baguette cut into slices and toasted

spreadable goat cheese

Optional: For a touch of creaminess add ⅓ cup hot heavy cream to finished soup.

In medium stockpot, heat olive oil on medium-high. Add onions and garlic. Cook for 5–6 minutes until translucent and soft. Add fresh vine-ripened tomatoes. Cook down for 20 minutes. Add balsamic vinegar, crushed tomatoes, chicken stock, red wine, and spices. Take stick blender, blender, or food processor and blend until smooth. Put back into pot if you use a food processor or blender. Let simmer for 45 minutes to an hour. If soup is too thick, add more chicken stock to thin out to your desired consistency. Add Parmesan cheese, mix in, and turn off heat. Season with salt and pepper. Take large round croutons and spread goat cheese on top.

STUFFED ITALIAN CHICKEN

This dish was a huge turning point in my life. I created this recipe for a few friends of mine when I was living in Kansas City. I was having a little get together at my house one evening and I wanted the night to be special. At this point in my life, I knew I loved to cook. But the thought of culinary school, prior to this recipe, had not even crossed my mind. Little did I know, I had a God-given talent for cooking. It all came to fruition after this recipe.

I wanted to prepare a meal that combined different textures and flavors, and I wanted to have fun doing it. This recipe was created from my own intuition and not a recipe book. I started out by marinating chicken in liquid smoke and beer. After marinating the chicken for several hours, I stuffed it with a mixture of ricotta cheese, spinach, goat cheese, red peppers, and a pinch of cinnamon. The idea for the cinnamon came from my Italian grandmother. She always told me that cinnamon puts a bit of "zing" in your food, especially bolognese sauce. This was important, she said, because you always want to surprise your guests' taste buds.

After the cheese mixture was set and stuffed into the chicken, I added to each chicken piece some sweet Italian peppers, sun dried tomatoes, and a few plump raisins, and then rolled them up and placed them in a baking dish with tomato sauce and red wine. My guests arrived just as the chicken was almost done, and the fabulous aroma filled my entire house.

I was thrilled when one of my friends commented to me that the aroma of the chicken reminded him of Garozzo's, the best Italian restaurant in Kansas City. As my guests sat down, I brought out the hot steamy creation and placed it in the center of the table. I served them and nervously awaited their first bites. As the compliments started rolling in, I felt at ease and proud of my accomplishments.

That very moment sparked my interested in the culinary arts. I had not realized how much I truly enjoyed cooking until I saw how much my guests were enjoying the dish I'd created. This particular meal is where it all started. It inspired me to pursue professional cooking.

After relishing the glory of this amazing dish, the gears started turning in my brain and I knew I had a passion to do something besides what I was currently doing. One evening as I sat at my computer desk, working away while food network was on in the background, my Aunt Carolyn called.

We had been talking for a brief while when she said something totally out of left field, "Why don't you go to culinary school?"

"What? Culinary school? Are you crazy?" I said. "I really don't know if I'm cut out for culinary school."

Well, six months after that conversation I wanted to find out whether or not I would like the "cooking" world. I had the opportunity through friends to work in a restaurant for a few nights. I worked in a mobile food truck, sold salsa, and continued to cook for my friends before deciding to apply to the Culinary Institute of America (CIA). The rest is history. In this book you will read all my other cockamamie stories confirming that this was the correct decision to make. I am so glad I followed my passion.

STUFFED ITALIAN CHICKEN

YIELD: 4 SERVINGS

4 chicken breasts, boneless, skinless

⅓ cup olive oil

salt and pepper

2 cups light beer

½ teaspoon liquid smoke (optional)

SAUCE

1 (28 oz.) can stewed tomatoes

⅓ cup red wine

1 tablespoon olive oil

salt and pepper

FILLING

1 cup ricotta cheese

⅓ cup cream cheese

2 tablespoons Parmesan cheese

1 teaspoon dried basil

½ teaspoon garlic salt

1 tablespoon dried parsley

½ teaspoon dried oregano

¼ teaspoon ground black pepper

⅛ teaspoon salt

⅓ cup raisins (golden and/or regular)

⅓ cup sun-dried tomatoes, packed in oil, chopped

⅓ cup roasted red peppers, chopped

GARNISH

Parmesan cheese

Preheat oven to 365 degrees.

Take each chicken breast and slice open in the middle from one side to the other, keeping the chicken hinged and attached. Brush chicken with olive oil. Season with salt and pepper. Place in baking dish and add beer (liquid smoke optional). Cover and set aside in fridge for 3–4 hours. If you want a more intense flavor, refrigerate overnight.

In medium bowl, place all filling ingredients. Mix well. Set aside in fridge.

In small bowl, place raisins, sun-dried tomatoes, and roasted red peppers. Mix together and set aside.

Remove chicken from marinade and pat dry with a paper towel. Discard marinade. Take each chicken breast and put 2–3 tablespoons of the filling inside the chicken. Make sure filling is evenly distributed. Add 2 tablespoons of pepper/raisin/sun-dried tomato mixture to each piece of chicken. Close opening with toothpicks (uncolored ones). Set pieces in a large glass baking dish.

In medium bowl add tomatoes, wine, and olive oil. Mix together and pour over chicken. Season to taste with salt and pepper.

Bake chicken for 35–45 minutes until chicken is completely cooked. Remove toothpicks before serving. Garnish with Parmesan cheese.

SCORE TIP:

STUFFED ITALIAN CHICKEN

What is liquid smoke? Liquid smoke is smoke produced through the controlled burning of wood chips or sawdust, condensed, and then passed through water, which captures and dissolves the smoke-flavored components in solution. Remember, with liquid smoke, a little bit goes along way. Too much liquid smoke in a dish could ruin it because of the concentrated smoke flavors. The substitute ingredients, if you can't find liquid smoke, are ground chipotle peppers and smoked paprika. Use half a teaspoon of each of these ingredients in place of liquid smoke.

Why use light beer instead of dark beer? Using light beer in this recipe will provide a very light flavor of the beer. You don't want to overpower this dish with the taste of a dark beer. Most keynote flavors in dark beer are deep chocolate, tobacco, yeast, and Worcestershire sauce. By using dark beer, you will overpower the true, authentic Italian flavors in this recipe. Light beer will not only provide the accents and undertones of a light hops flavor, but will also blend these amazing ingredients together.

If you have a gluten allergy or intolerance, use gluten-free beer or omit the beer and do not marinate chicken.

STOKER SALSA

After making the amazing stuffed chicken dish, the fire in my internal oven had been sparked and I knew my true passion: cooking. This is what led me to start my own salsa business.

I first came up with this recipe when I was living in Kansas City. I was working in the television industry and culinary school was just a thought simmering in the back of my mind. One evening I watched Food Network, which featured a story on various hot chili peppers from Mexico. So, with a thousand recipe ideas in my head, I started thinking about making my own salsa. I decided to experiment in my little kitchen with various chilis and tomatoes. And lo and behold, Stoker Salsa was created.

I asked all my friends in the Kansas City area to try my salsa and they absolutely loved it. But almost everyone asked, "Ummm, what is that distinctive flavor in there?" While experimenting, I added a few secret ingredients—ingredients that aren't found in your typical salsa.

Martin, who was my boyfriend at the time, talked me into selling my salsa at the local farmers' market. He went downtown to the government offices and obtained a business license for me. He then paid the fee for the stall space, and we were ready to sell. To this day, he swears that he designed all the labels to fit around the salsa jars, but I know I played a very integral part in the design. I wanted to use some funky-shaped jars to house the salsa. I didn't want your ordinary, typical salsa jar. I searched everywhere in Kansas City and somehow stumbled upon this beekeeper store that had the most amazing glass containers. Not only did I find glass containers that were cheap and unique, I learned that bee-keeping was an extensive hobby. As I made my selection, the owner of the store boxed all my containers, wrapped them in cute bee paper, and gave me a bag of free honey samples, and I was on my way back to the kitchen to start the salsa-making process. My grass roots business, Stoker Salsa, was coming together

and the next day at the market would be the start of something great.

I prepared all the salsa in my kitchen that night and when I was finished at 1:00 a.m., the place looked as if an M80 had gone off. My boyfriend was fast asleep in my comfy bed, oblivious to the strident kitchen noises I was creating and the violent rain storm going on. I finally went to bed, and when my head hit the pillow, my alarm went off. The clock showed 4:30 a.m., and I desperately needed my coffee fix. Martin started loading the salsa into the car.

I was in the shower when he came bursting into the bathroom and said, "What happened last night? There are trees down everywhere."

I said, "You didn't hear that crazy-ass storm last night?"

Apparently he didn't care at this point about the aftermath of the storm because all of a sudden he was fully in the buff and in the shower with me. Our five-minute "quickie" in the hot, steamy shower really woke us both up. As my heart rate came down and I got dressed, Martin loaded the rest of the car with the remainder of the Stoker Salsa, signs, banners, extra cash, and business cards. We started to make our way downtown. As we rounded the corner of our apartment complex, we saw three massive fire trucks blocking the entrance/exit. Lights were flashing. About a dozen firefighters were walking around. There were police cars, ambulances—what on earth was going on? All I could see was the front entrance blocked by this monstrosity of a truck and I had to get to the farmers' market for my big debut. Apparently lightning had struck one of the massive trees in my complex and set one of the units on fire.

"What a fucking mess this is. How the hell are we going to get out?" I said in a major panic. "Do something. Go move that fire truck."

Martin looked at me as if I had four heads and said,

"And how am I going to do that, Jenn?"

"Tell them we need to get out of here. This is an emergency."

Two firefighters came up to our window and said, "You need to back away from this area, sir."

Martin said, "We need to get out of the complex."

The firefighter said, "Not for at least forty-five minutes. We have to get the fire under control and the area secure."

What were we going to do? I was going to be late for my salsa debut and miss my window of opportunity. I was in tears when Martin said, "Let's try something."

He drove his SUV up the grassy, wooded hill. We destroyed a few trees and shrubs, but we finally made it to the street. All I could see in the rearview mirror were a few firefighters shaking their heads at what we had just done. But hey, you gotta do what ya gotta do, right? As we arrived, the sun was just cresting the horizon. The farmers and other vendors were unloading their produce and the fog and thick rain clouds were lifting off the city. The smell of sweet candied nuts, fresh earthy produce, fried dough, and chocolate filled the air. We spotted our space and started to set up the salsa display. I was lacking marketing materials, but we set out samples, and I was sure they would get the patrons hooked. The salsa was a hit. Everyone who came by had nothing but good things to say. Even though I broke even in sales, I still had a blast. This experience along with many that you will read about in the following pages, led me to pursue my passion in life. The next year, I enrolled at the Culinary Institute of America in New York.

STOKER SALSA

4 vine-ripened tomatoes, chopped

1 (15 oz.) can stewed tomatoes

1 teaspoon balsamic vinegar

⅓ cup fresh cilantro, stems removed, chopped

1 tablespoon fresh jalapeño, seeds and white pith removed, chopped

½ teaspoon fresh garlic, chopped

1 teaspoon olive oil

1 lime, juiced

salt and pepper

1 teaspoon ground cumin

pinch of red pepper flakes

Blend the vine-ripened tomatoes in blender or food processor until consistency is chunky, not smooth. Add the rest of the ingredients and blend until all is incorporated. Add salt and pepper to taste. Refrigerate for several hours before severing. Serve with your favorite tortilla chips.

MY AHA MOMENT

Little did I know I was walking toward my culinary dream during those years in Kansas City. Many things were generated from the simple idea of selling my Stoker Salsa at the farmers' market.

Let me take you back to my early childhood. I always had an entrepreneurial spirit. I remember starting a door-to-door cookie business with my cousin when I was ten years old. We called it Kinfer Cookies

(Jennifer and Kindra combined). We premade four kinds of cookie dough and went door-to-door taking orders for fresh, homemade cookies. After collecting all the orders, we went to the freezer, scooped out the type of dough that our customers had specified, baked the cookies, and put them in white bags with the hand-written logo, Kinfer Cookies. I think I had the drive to succeed at early age and that drive started to grow to a new level in Kansas City. In my first career in the film and television business, I had the drive to succeed at anything I did. I would go that extra mile and work for pennies just to get all the experience I could.

When I was first out of college, I worked for a wireless phone company. I went with one of my coworkers to an audition for a role in an independent film that they were shooting in downtown Kansas City. It was a nonpaying role, but my coworker wanted to get more exposure in the film business. I went with her for moral support. As we waited for her turn to audition, we went across the street to guzzle a few cocktails so her nerves would calm. When we went back to the audition, I ended up auditioning—drunk, mind you—and I landed the starring role in the thirty-minute film. How the hell did I manage that one? Who knows? My friend was not too happy with me.

After that event, I started to pursue the vocational area I had graduated in: television. I worked at a couple of local news stations, doing behind-the-scenes work, camera, chyron, and teleprompter. That led to working for a local government TV channel, and I ended up in sports TV production. Along the way, though, many things sparked my interest in the culinary world. I had no idea how I learned to do the things I did. I had a natural-born culinary talent. For instance, Martin and I worked out with this insane Russian personal trainer who made an NFL linebacker look minuscule. His favorite lines to say to us—of course in his thick Russian accent—were, "That pain you're feeling right now is all that weakness and it's leaving your body," and "The only good day was yesterday." Really? Quotes to live by, I guess.

The Russian had both of us on a very strict high-protein diet that was not the best tasting. He wasn't a chef and didn't care that the food tasted plain. He wanted us to get as much protein as possible regardless of the taste. The menu line-up was as follows: plain canned tuna, canned chicken, boiled eggs, plain white rice . . . and the dreaded food list goes on. So, I took the initiative and tried to spice up our meals without adding extra calories and fat. To the canned chicken we had to eat I added salsa, spices, fresh tomatoes, and jalapeños. I turned a mundane, not-so-good thing into something that tasted pretty dam good. I whipped the hard-boiled egg yolks with roasted red pepper hummus and made low fat/calorie deviled eggs. To the canned tuna, I added mustard, plain yogurt, onions, chili powder, and lime juice, and it was off-the-charts good. To satisfy the sweet tooth, I made muffins and instead of oil, I used apple sauce to maintain the consistency and moisture content.

As I became more interested in the culinary world, I conjured up my own cooking show pilot. I was working for a local Kansas City public access TV station and I wanted to add more spice (no pun intended) to the watching-grass-grow show line-up. I wanted to create a show that focused on healthy eating and the people who made a difference with food. I put together a script, interviewed a handful of local foodies, and was ready to take my crew and film to the studio for shots. But as luck had it, within the nine months of putting the show together, I applied to the best culinary school in United States, the CIA, was accepted, and pursued my dream. So the moral of the story is: No one, no matter what their age or where they are in life, should let their passion pass them by. Go for it, because it will probably be the best thing you have ever done. It truly has been an amazing adventure and the journey still continues.

Feeding That Man's Heart and Stomach
Well... Just Temporarily

Chapter 2

The Ex's

Wine Cooler Chicken

Stuffed Chicken Paillard

Fennel, Cucumber, Endive, Radicchio Salad with Citrus-Sesame Vinaigrette, Drizzled with Lavender Honey

Herb-Scented Lobster Tails

Filet Mignon Wrapped in Bacon with Sherry-Balsamic Glaze

Butternut Squash-Sage Puree

Garlic Spinach with Seared Herb Tomatoes

Pumpkin Cheesecake with Sugar Cookie Crust

Lobster Risotto

Lobster Stock

Kenny's Baked Stuffed Clams (World Famous)

Bruschetta

Cucumber Cups with Mediterranean Salad Filling

Roasted Red Pepper and Caponata Hummus

Barbeque-Potato-Chip-Encrusted Sea Scallops with Leek, Fennel, and Mushroom Ragout

Stoker Pickled Red Onions and Jalapeños

Lobster Panzanella Salad

Barbeque Lobster Quesadilla

Looking Good and Feeling Good Martini

Fried Plantains Topped with Chipotle-Cinnamon Pulled Pork and Jicama Salsa

Parmesan Baskets Filled with Caesar Salad and Croutons

Chayote Salsa

Cinnamon-Chipotle-Barbeque Chicken Wings and Yogurt Cucumber Sauce

Grilled Lamb with Asian Pesto, Thai Cabbage Slaw, and Coconut-Lemon Sauce

Moroccan-Caribbean Chicken Stew with Cilantro-Jasmine Rice

Moroccan-Mexican Chicken Stew over Basmati Rice

Japanese Citrus Salmon with Soba Noodles and Sautéed Garlic Bok Choy

Tuscan-Style Rigatoni with Braised Tomatoes, Spinach, and Italian Sausage in a Light Tomato-Broth Sauce

Fresh Herb-Encrusted Lamb Chops with Mint-Pea Puree and

Rosemary-Tomato Couscous

No-Joke Smoked Chicken Chili

Roasted Red Pepper and Sun-Dried Tomato Bruschetta with Toasted Pine-Nut Puree, Topped with Goat Cheese Gremolata

Ginger, Tomato, Citrus Shredded Flank Steak with Pancetta Black Beans

Thai Coconut Chicken Soup

Stoker Shrimp Cakes with Hearts of Palm-Avocado Salad and Creole Mustard Vinaigrette

Tator Tot Nachos

Cotton Candy Martini

THESE RECIPES WERE CREATED FOR THE MANY MEN THAT FILTERED IN AND OUT OF MY LIFE.

"The way to a man's heart is through his stomach." Well, sometimes that's not the case. As my lifelong love journey still continues, I have yet to find "the one." Hopefully he's right around the corner. The road has been full of good times and bad. I now consider myself a professional dater and have dated every type of man under the sun. These stories and recipes reflect the men that came in and out of my life.

In life things happen for a reason, and I'm a firm believer that people come in and out of your life for a purpose. Every man I have ever dated taught me something different about myself and life in general. The recipes that came from these relationships show how much passion I had for these men and the food I prepared for them. I am truly blessed that these relationships helped inspire my creations. I created some pretty damn good recipes. Thanks guys. I knew you were good for something.

Note: names in the following stories have been changed to protect the innocent.

Ex Number One

Bill and...

Wine Cooler Chicken

Stuffed Chicken Paillard

Fennel, Cucumber, Endive, Radicchio Salad with Citrus-Sesame Vinaigrette, Drizzled with Lavender Honey

Herb-Scented Lobster Tails

Filet Mignon Wrapped in Bacon with Sherry-Balsamic Glaze

Butternut Squash-Sage Puree

Garlic Spinach with Seared Herb Tomatoes

Pumpkin Cheesecake with Sugar Cookie Crust

A little bit about Bill: his favorite food was spaghetti and meatballs from a can. His favorite restaurants were Denny's and White Castle, and his idea of a nice night out was at his favorite, local Connecticut tavern. Bill was a state trooper and he liked the basics in life. Bill had two kids from a previous marriage that had gone very sour. He worked very hard to provide a great life for them and was a committed father. I was new to Connecticut and Bill was the first person I really dated. I was not sure what the guys were like in C town, but Bill seemed to have a quirky cuteness about him. Besides, the guy looked so hot in his police uniform when I first met him I was ready to head back to his squad car and have my way with him. On our first date, we met for coffee after Bill got off his patrol shift. I knew right away who he was: full police uniform, buzz haircut, and smiling from ear to ear. He extended his arms to give me a big bear hug. I felt his thick bullet-proof vest press into my chest and his 9mm gun in its holster brushed my hip ever so slightly. Not only did his rough and tough image turn me on, he was nice, soft spoken, and kind. I was in love.

On our second date, Bill picked me up in his non-police car and said we were heading to his house for dinner. Wow! A sexy cop that can cook? We pulled into his driveway and drove through a forest of trees up to a large, white, colonial home. He told me it was his parent's house and he was living there temporarily. My brain was saying, "What, you live with your parents? You're a cop and a grown-ass man for the love of God." Now the man in uniform didn't appear so hot anymore. How lovely, I thought as we walked through the garage to head inside. As he opened the door, I saw the whole family in the kitchen: parents, sister, her husband, kids, and the grandmother. Bill took the initiative and introduced me. What a second date, huh? Bill's mother immediately asked if I wanted anything to drink, and I said, "Yes. Do you have any wine?" I needed it to calm my nerves, but dinner was great. I never felt so at home.

His mom and I became instant friends and she quickly recruited me as the "celebrity" chef of their family. On our third date, Bill and I headed back to his parents' house and I made a lobster feast for his whole family—fourteen people. On the menu that evening was lobster panzanella and lobster risotto. All the men in the family helped me set up the massive turkey fryer in the front yard so we could cook all twelve lobsters. We filled it with water, added kosher salt, and started the F-16 engine to heat the water. The little crustaceans were trapped in their Igloo Cooler tomb waiting for their hot-water bath. As the men took care of the lobsters, I headed inside to get everyone ready for the main event. We covered the large center island with newspaper and set out a few large glass bowls and lobster claw crackers. The hot, bright red, steamy lobsters were brought in and set in the middle of the island for everyone to start the lobster dissection. I taught them all how to break down the cooked lobsters and get the most meat out of the shells. Bill's eighty-eight-year-old grandmother was covered in lobster juice and had pieces of lobster meat lodged in her hair. It was like a scene out of a movie. I've never heard so much laughter and seen so many smiles in all my life.

As we continued our journey together for the next several months, the only thing that Bill and I had in common were our hot, steamy extracurricular activities in the bedroom. As I stated in the beginning, it's so true what they say about a man in uniform, especially when he puts on a police uniform and comes over to your house after a long, hard day of fighting crime. Mama mia! It was sexy as hell. As the "uniform" hotness wore off, I think in the end I was more attached to his family than I was to him. Bill's mom even confronted me at one point at one of our many dinner parties and told me that she didn't think this was the kind of relationship I was looking for. I was a little taken aback but could see the writing on the wall. Bill just wasn't the person I was looking for, and we decided to go our separate ways.

I remained friends with his mom and catered numerous parties for her thereafter. It was a little weird at first, but I quickly I got over it when I received the check.

The first party I catered for Bill's mother was a

Red Hatter's meeting. I made my berry wine cooler chicken wrapped in prosciutto. This recipe came on a whim. I had forgotten to marinate the chicken the night before and when my friend Kim and I arrived at Bill's parent's house, we searched for some type of marinade ingredient in her fridge. Without many options, I grabbed a wild berry wine cooler that I saw, opened the bottle, and poured it over the chicken to marinate for several hours. After the chicken got nice and drunk in the marinade, I wrapped each chicken piece in thinly sliced, salty prosciutto, put them in the baking dish, and baked them with a tangy marinara sauce. After they baked and all the salty, sweet, and tangy flavors mingled together, the taste was unbelievable. It was the best chicken I had ever tasted. The layers of flavor danced so perfectly across my tongue. It was a match made in heaven. Who would have thought a wine cooler, a beverage I used to drink in high school and college, would make a piece of chicken taste out of this world? This dish was a hit among all the Red Hatter ladies. They liked it so much they made me an honorary member of their Red Hatter group (even though I wasn't sixty-five-plus years old).

WINE COOLER CHICKEN

YIELD: 4 SERVINGS

4 chicken breasts, skinless, boneless

1 (28 oz.) canned stewed tomatoes

½ cup blush or red wine

½ teaspoon sugar

¼ teaspoon garlic salt

1 tablespoon olive oil

¼ teaspoon ground black pepper

½ lb. prosciutto, sliced thin

salt and pepper to taste

MARINADE

1 bottle berry wine cooler

1 teaspoon salt

pinch pepper

1 tablespoon Italian seasoning

1 tablespoon balsamic vinegar

2 tablespoons olive oil

¼ teaspoon ground rosemary

1 Ziploc bag

Combine chicken, wine cooler, salt, pepper, Italian seasoning, vinegar, rosemary, and oil in the Ziploc bag. Zip tight and shake until all ingredients are blended. Put in fridge for 2–3 hours. For more intense flavor, marinate overnight.

In baking dish, add canned tomatoes, wine, sugar, garlic salt, olive oil and pepper. Mix together. Take chicken and remove from Ziploc bag. Discard marinade. Take a few slices of the prosciutto and wrap around each chicken breast. Put chicken in baking dish, on top of marinara sauce, and bake for 35–45 minutes at 350 degrees or until chicken is completely cooked.

SCORE TIP:

WINE COOLER CHICKEN

Even though the alcohol will cook out during the baking process, if you do not want to use alcohol in this recipe, replace the wine cooler with ½ cup tonic water and ¾ cup grape juice. This will produce the same delicious berry flavor throughout the recipe.

SAUCE SUBSTITUTE: replace the red wine with ¼ cup cranberry juice, ¼ cup grape juice, and 1 tablespoon balsamic vinegar.

If prosciutto is going to break your budget for this recipe, replace it with par cooked bacon, one or two small slices per chicken piece.

The second party I catered for Bill's mother was her niece's wedding shower. I cooked for forty people, all by myself. I made stuffed chicken paillard; fennel, cucumber, endive, and radicchio salad with citrus vinaigrette; and Mediterranean brown rice salad.

SCORE TIP:

STUFFED CHICKEN PAILLARD

You're probably asking what on earth a paillard is. Well, it's a fancy name for meat—chicken, steak, veal, pork, etc.—that has been pounded and flattened with a meat mallet until it's very thin. Why turn a piece of protein into a paillard? So you can stuff the meat. Using the paillard technique, you will achieve successfully stuffed protein.

stuffed chicken paillard

STUFFED CHICKEN PAILLARD

YIELD: 4 SERVINGS

4 boneless, skinless chicken breasts

1 bunch asparagus, fibrous ends removed

1 small log goat cheese

½ pound sliced prosciutto

whole basil leaves

2 tablespoons olive oil

salt

pepper

1 tablespoon lemon juice

½ cup chicken broth

1 tablespoon butter

toothpicks

GARNISH

fresh, chopped basil

Place a sheet of plastic wrap across cutting board. Place one piece of chicken breast in center. Place another piece of plastic wrap on top. With meat mallet pound each piece of chicken breast until thin. Make sure chicken is not too thin. Repeat until all chicken is pounded. Stack on top of one another, keeping flattened chicken between the plastic wraps.

Cut fibrous ends off asparagus. Bring medium-sized pot of salted water to boil. Add asparagus and cook until 75 percent done (3–4 minutes). Take out of boiling water and shock in ice water. Take out of water, drain, and reserve.

Remove plastic wrap from chicken and put 2 tablespoons goat cheese in center of each flattened chicken; spread evenly.

Layer 2–3 slices of prosciutto on top of goat cheese and then lay 3–4 asparagus sprigs, with ends hanging over the side, and top with a few fresh basil leaves. Roll chicken and tuck ends in. Secure with toothpicks if necessary. Season with salt and pepper.

Heat medium sauté pan and add 2 tablespoons olive oil. When pan is very hot, put chicken rolls in pan and sear on both sides until golden brown, approximately 4–5 minutes per side. Add chicken broth and lemon juice to bottom of pan. Put whole sauté pan in oven and finish cooking at 350 degrees for 15–20 minutes or until chicken is thoroughly cooked. Take out of oven and add butter to liquid; mix together. Serve with lemon crème fraiche sauce and top with chopped basil.

FENNEL, CUCUMBER, ENDIVE, RADICCHIO SALAD WITH CITRUS-SESAME VINAIGRETTE, DRIZZLED WITH LAVENDER HONEY

YIELD: 4 SERVINGS

2 fennel bulbs, top, bottom and core removed, sliced thin

1 seedless cucumber, sliced into ¼-inch-thick half circles (Use cucumbers that have the plastic wrappers.)

2 endives, ends removed, cut into small pieces

1 radicchio head, core removed, sliced thin (or ¼ whole red cabbage, sliced thin)

1 red pepper, seeds and core removed, chopped

⅓ cup green onion, sliced thin

1 cup shiitake mushrooms, stems removed, sliced thin

2 cups button mushrooms, stems removed, sliced thin

2 tablespoons olive oil

¼ cup balsamic vinegar

2 tablespoons capers

DRESSING

2 tablespoons lemon juice, fresh

⅓ cup apple cider vinegar

1 teaspoon yellow mustard

1 tablespoon honey

⅛ teaspoon Salt

pinch ground black pepper

dash hot sauce

½ teaspoon sesame oil (optional)

⅓ cup olive oil

GARNISH

honey

1 tablespoon dried lavender

(optional)

In medium sauté pan, heat 2 tablespoons olive oil. Add mushrooms and sauté on medium heat, 7–9 minutes. Add balsamic vinegar and cook until mushrooms are soft and there is no liquid in the pan. Take off heat and allow mushrooms to cool on plate. Cut all other ingredients and put into large bowl. When mushroom mixture has cooled completely, add to rest of the vegetables.

In small bowl, add all dressing ingredients except for olive oil. Whisk together until all ingredients are incorporated. Whisk in olive oil slowly. Drizzle over vegetable mixture and toss until all ingredients are coated. Drizzle honey on salad and serve immediately.

Optional: Crush dried lavender in honey and mix before drizzling over salad.

WHAT IS AN ENGLISH CUCUMBER?

I really like to use this type of cucumber because they are seedless, have a more delicate, greener skin, produce less water content than regular cucumbers, and have a milder taste. They are sometimes marketed as "burpless." The seeds and skin of the other variety of cucumber can give some people gas.

They might not be for everyone, but they are very easy to prepare. Just peel down the plastic covering, wash, and chop away.

If shiitake mushrooms are a little too earthy and/or too expensive for your taste, replace them with white, button mushrooms. Use a total of 3 cups.

Did you know that mustard used in vinaigrette acts as an emulsifier? This ingredient not only binds and stabilizes the vinaigrette but adds a bold depth of flavor. Additional emulsifier ingredients that will bring added flavor and texture are roasted, mashed garlic; egg; honey; fruit and vegetable purees.

If you are sensitive to acid, try adding a tablespoon of milk or cream to your vinaigrette. This will help smooth out the acidity of the vinegar.

LAVENDER HONEY: If you are true foodie, lavender honey is a great garnish for this particular recipe

fennel, cucumber, endive, radicchio salad with citrus sesame-vinaigrette, drizzled with lavender honey

The last event I catered for Bill's mother was a going-away party for her best friends, who were moving to Florida. The menu included herb-scented lobster tails, filet mignon wrapped in bacon with a sherry and balsamic glaze, butternut squash puree, garlic spinach, and seared herb tomatoes. For dessert, I made my pumpkin cheesecake with a sugar-cookie crust and homemade amaretto whipped cream.

This was a very interesting party because, at the time, Bill and I had been separated for four months and I was bringing the guy I was currently dating to be my sous chef. The flavor of the month, Trevor, whom I had just started dating, was a food and wine expert on top of being a successful entrepreneur. He traveled to exotic places and knew a little bit about a lot of things. I knew the crowd would love him. The only thing I wasn't forthcoming about was where we were cooking. I didn't tell Trevor that we were at my exboyfriend's parents' house. I had some big cojones to pull a move like this: bringing my current beau to my ex's parent's house where my ex still lived and not telling my current beau what the situation was. Yes, I know, seriously, very wrong and disturbing, but oh, what a rush! All in all, the evening went very well. It was a little uncomfortable in the beginning but nothing I couldn't handle. Having a few cocktails throughout the evening made all my fears melt away. Thank God for a good glass of vino! Ah, mama mia!

HERB-SCENTED LOBSTER TAILS

YIELD: 4 SERVINGS

4 lobster tails (½–¾ pound)

8–10 small to medium-sized flat rocks

¼ bunch of fresh parsley

3 sprigs rosemary

3 sprigs sage

3 large cloves garlic, halved

½ cup white wine

water

Clean rocks under cold water. Line bottom of large stockpot with rocks. Add water and wine until it barely covers rocks. Put all herbs and garlic on top of rocks. Heat pot on high until liquid boils. Lay lobster tails on rocks, close with lid, and allow to steam for 7–9 minutes or until lobster is completely done. Serve hot.

SCORE TIP:

LOBSTER TAILS

When buying frozen lobster tails, you should always buy from a fish market that is well known for selling high-quality seafood. Lobster tails range in size from 2 oz. to as large as 24 oz. Lobster tails may be cooked from a frozen state. However, your best results are achieved if the tails are defrosted. To defrost in the safest, most efficient way, place the tails in the fridge for 12–24 hours.

There are many types of lobster species available in your local markets today. A lot of people really don't know the difference between the species and assume that the taste is similar. This is not the case. Lobsters from cold waters are mainly found in Maine, New Zealand, South Africa, and Australia, and are considered the highest quality. This type of lobster is more expensive, but you will almost always be guaranteed high-quality lobster meat. The reason why cold-water lobsters are superior in quality is because lobsters grown in this environment take longer to age. Cold-water lobsters grow bigger over time and develop more flavors underneath their shells.

The lobsters from warmer waters are found in the Caribbean, Mediterranean, Asia, and Florida. They are similar to cold-water lobsters, but instead of claws, they have long spiny antennae. The only edible meat in a warm-water lobster is found in the tail. Warm-water lobsters are sometimes called spiny or rock lobsters. They are cheaper than cold-water lobsters, and often, they are the frozen lobster tails you find in your local markets. The taste and quality in my opinion does not measure up to that of their cold-water counterparts. So, if you're preparing an impressive meal for a captive audience, do not serve warm-water lobster.

When warm-water lobster tails are old or have gone bad, the lobster meat may remain mushy after cooking and fall apart when eaten or give off a pungent smell of ammonia.

Herb-scented lobster tails: Cooking on flat rocks is a great technique when steaming any type of shellfish, especially lobster tails. The best rocks to use are the flat ocean or river rocks. If you cannot find them, try to obtain the flattest rocks possible. If you purchase the rocks, do not buy the chemically treated ones. Thoroughly clean the rocks before cooking with them. Take a very large stockpot and line the bottom with the rocks. Fill with water until it crests the top of the rocks. Add your herbs, garlic, and a few splashes of white wine. Bring to a boil. Place lobster tails on top of rocks and cover pot with lid. Steam until lobster tails are fully cooked.

FILET MIGNON WRAPPED IN BACON WITH SHERRY-BALSAMIC GLAZE

YIELD: 4 SERVINGS

4 raw filet mignons, 5–6 oz. each

4 full strips bacon

salt and pepper

2 tablespoons Worcestershire sauce

2 tablespoons olive oil

GARNISH

goat cheese crumbles

Season filets with salt and pepper on both sides. Cook bacon in pan until 50 percent done. Remove from pan and allow to cool. Wrap each filet with bacon and hold together with toothpicks.

Top each one with Worcestershire sauce and olive oil. Bake in oven at 450 degrees until desired doneness. Top with sherry and balsamic glaze and goat cheese.

SCORE TIP:

FILET MIGNON WRAPPED IN BACON

For best cooking results with your filet, before putting it into a hot oven or onto a hot grill, allow the steak to come to room temp. There are two reasons for this: a cold steak will contract when it hits a high-heat source and this will cause it to toughen. Also, a steak that is cold in the center and at room temperature on the surface will not cook evenly. You will have a cold center and a nice sear on the outside. So your best bet is to remove the steaks from the fridge at least 30 minutes before cooking them. Pat them completely dry with a paper towel before cooking, or you will, essentially, steam them.

SHERRY-BALSAMIC GLAZE

YIELD: 4 SERVINGS

1 cup balsamic vinegar

½ cup sherry vinegar

2 tablespoons honey

½ teaspoon thyme, chopped

salt and pepper

2 tablespoons apricot jam

In medium saucepan, mix all ingredients and bring to a rolling boil.

Reduce heat slightly, and still allow to boil. Reduce mixture to ½–⅓ cup. It should be slightly thick. Allow to cool for 15 minutes. Drizzle over filet mignons.

BUTTERNUT SQUASH-SAGE PUREE

YIELD: 4 – 6 SERVINGS

2 medium butternut squashes, split in half, seeds scooped out

⅓ cup olive oil

salt and pepper

2 tablespoons sage leaves, chopped

¼ cup white wine

½ cup water

sage stems

2 tablespoons butter

½ cup heavy cream

2 tablespoons Parmesan cheese

Brush butternut squash with olive oil and sprinkle with salt, pepper, and sage. Add white wine and water to baking dish. Lay butternut squash facing up in dish, skin side down.

Bake at 375 degrees for 45 minutes to one hour or until the butternut squash is soft and golden brown.

When butternut squash has cooled enough to handle, scoop out the flesh with a spoon and place in blender or food processor, discarding the skin. Blend until smooth. In medium saucepan on medium-low heat, add butternut squash puree, butter, and heavy cream. Stir until blended. Allow to cook for 8–10 minutes. Add Parmesan cheese and turn off heat. Season to taste with salt and pepper. Serve hot.

SCORE TIP:

BUTTERNUT SQUASH-SAGE PUREE

Want to make this dairy free or want to cut some calories and fat? Replace the butter with 2 tablespoons of soy butter or any type of dairy-free butter. Replace the heavy cream with ½ cup softened vegan soy cream cheese or fat-free cream cheese and the Parmesan cheese, which you can keep because it is very low in lactose and fat. If you want to keep this dish completely dairy free, use vegan soy Parmesan cheese. (You can find this product at your nearest natural/organic market.)

GARLIC SPINACH WITH SEARED HERB TOMATOES

YIELD: 4 SERVINGS

6-8 cups spinach, packed tightly

2 tablespoons olive oil

2 teaspoons garlic, chopped

1 pint cherry tomatoes

2 teaspoons dried basil

1 teaspoon dried oregano

¼ teaspoon black pepper

¼ teaspoon red pepper flakes

1 teaspoon garlic salt

salt

In large sauté pan, heat olive oil on medium-high. Add garlic and cook for 1 minute. Add cherry tomatoes and incorporate olive oil and garlic. Add all spices and coat tomatoes. Cook for 5–7 minutes. Start adding spinach in batches until spinach cooks down. Repeat until all spinach is cooked down and liquid is almost gone. Mix ingredients together. Season with salt and pepper. Serve hot.

PUMPKIN CHEESECAKE WITH SUGAR COOKIE CRUST

YIELD: 8 – 10 SERVINGS

CRUST

2 cups sugar cookies, crushed

1 cup cashews

½ stick butter, melted

⅓ cup sugar

PUMPKIN FILLING

3 packages cream cheese, 1 light, 2 regular

4 eggs

1 ¼ cups pumpkin filling

¼ cup heavy cream

¼ cup honey

1 teaspoon vanilla

¼ teaspoon salt

¼ teaspoon cinnamon

⅛ teaspoon nutmeg

⅛ teaspoon all-spice

½ cup sugar

Preheat oven to 350 degrees. Use a 9 ½-inch to 10-inch spring-form pan.

To make crust: finely grind cookies, cashews, and sugar in food processor. Add melted butter and blend until combined. Press crust mixture onto bottom and up sides of spring-form pan. Bake for 10 minutes and then remove from oven and allow to cool slightly.

In another bowl, add cream cheese. With electric mixer, beat in eggs one at a time until all is incorporated. Add pumpkin filling, heavy cream, vanilla, salt, sugar, and spices. Blend together until smooth.

Pour filling into crust. Bake until cheesecake puffs, top browns, and center moves only slightly when pan is shaken. Takes about 1 hour. Transfer cheesecake to rack and cool.

SCORE TIP:

PUMPKIN CHEESECAKE

Not a fan of cashews? Replace with toasted pecans, toasted walnuts, or hazelnuts. Use the same amount: 1 cup. Or, to make this completely nut free, just increase the sugar cookie amount to a total of 3 cups. You also can use oatmeal cookies, gingersnaps, or butter cookies.

Ex Number Two

Edward and...

Lobster Risotto

Lobster Stock

Kenny's Baked Stuffed Clams (World Famous)

After graduating from CIA, I started working for a restaurant/hospitality company in New York. When I first started, I commuted every day from upstate New York to White Plains because I hadn't found a place to live that was close to the office. Another coworker of mine introduced me to Edward, the president of the company. After we had talked for a while, he suggested a few places to live that were close to the office and had semi affordable prices. I wanted to know what he meant by "affordable" because I was sure money was no object for him since he was the president of the company. So I took his lovely advice and went on an apartment hunt because, God knows, I couldn't afford a house; I ruled that out. Lo and behold, after a week of searching, I finally found an apartment.

A week after moving into my beautiful apartment, I was still talking to Edward on a daily basis in the office. I found out that Edward liked to run, so we decided to meet one night after work for a brisk five-mile run. Was this a good idea? Running with the president of my company? I'm not going to lie. I was very apprehensive about this and didn't know if it was appropriate. But after twenty minutes of feeling every unnerving apprehension under the sun, all the emotions suddenly melted away like an ice cube in a hot cup of coffee. I said to myself, "What the hell!" and went for it.

Edward and I continued to run together a few times a week for a straight month. Our runs became fun because we didn't talk business. We really got to know one another on a personal level. I saw a side of him that was completely different from the office side. We had an odd but good chemistry between the two of us and when he kissed me unexpectedly after one of our runs, I could feel the electricity shoot throughout my entire body. After that moment, we were inseparable. The only dark side to this relationship, though, was the fact that we had to keep this a secret at the office and not reveal to anyone

the honest, true facts of our relationship. It was very hard to keep the secret among my coworkers/friends, but I knew what the repercussions would be, so I kept it under lock and key. Edward and I would pass each other in the hall and not even say hello. Then five minutes later, he would call my office and say hello, even though he was ten feet down the hallway. He even sent a massive bouquet of flowers to the office one day (ballsy move) and signed it with a different name. He used the initials SHP (translation: Smoking Hot Pants). Everyone at the office was very inquisitive as to who the mystery man was in my life.

During those six months when we dated, he helped inspire a few of my creations, including my lobster risotto and lobster stock. I showed him how to use lobster shells to make a fortified lobster stock. After the stock was made, I showed him the proper way to make a risotto. The one thing I said to him over and over was, "Ya gotta be there for the risotto." The risotto process takes twenty-two minutes exactly and you have to babysit it like a two-year-old child.

Along the way, Edward introduced me to his crazy friends Kenny and Lisa. Kenny was a true New Yorker who loved to drink wine and indulge in good food regularly. Lisa was a very quiet girl who needed a wardrobe refresh, head-to-toe make-over, and once dated Edward. Kenny was a novice chef, and he liked to cook in his spare time. He had a few recipes up his sleeve to try to trump me the night he met me. He showed me how to make his famous stuffed clams. All I can say is that he and his clam recipe are truly legendary. It's gastronomic greatness.

After six months, things didn't end well for Edward and me because he rekindled his relationship with his long-loved ex. This story has a twist, though. Edward went back to dating his beloved ex and eventually proposed to her. Six months later, she dumped him, gave back the three-carat ring, got pregnant by another guy, and gave birth to her child on Edward's birthday. Did ya follow that?

lobster risotto

LOBSTER RISOTTO

YIELD: 4 SERVINGS

2 (1 lb.) lobsters, cooked and meat removed, shells set aside

2 tablespoons olive oil

½ teaspoon fresh garlic, chopped

½ cup yellow onion, diced small

½ cup leeks, finely chopped

⅓ cup red peppers, diced small

1 pound risotto rice

hot lobster stock, as needed

white wine, as needed

⅓ cup Parmesan cheese

1 tablespoon butter

salt and pepper to taste

In a medium pot, heat olive oil on medium-high. Add garlic, onions, leeks, and peppers. Cook for 7–8 minutes and lower heat to medium. Cook until onions are translucent and peppers are soft. Add rice and mix all ingredients together. Cook until rice is slightly toasted, about 6–8 minutes. Add hot lobster stock in increments, a few ladles at a time, continually stirring. When risotto has absorbed liquid, add a little bit more stock, and continually keep adding liquid in increments. When risotto is almost done (al dente), add a couple splashes of wine. Add Parmesan cheese, butter, and lobster meat. Mix together for 1 minute and turn off heat. Serve in bowls. Garnish with chopped chives or parsley.

LOBSTER STOCK

YIELD: 4 SERVINGS

lobster shells, meat removed

1 tablespoon tomato paste

1 teaspoon fresh garlic, chopped

½ cup carrots, chopped

¾ cup yellow onions, chopped

½ cup celery, chopped

⅓ cup parsley, stems and leaves, chopped

½ cup leeks, chopped large

1 cup white wine

water

salt and pepper to taste

GARNISH

chopped chives or parsley

In large stockpot, heat olive oil on high. Add lobster shells. Cook for 10–12 minutes on high heat until shells are a light golden brown. Add tomato paste. Reduce heat to medium-high and cook for 3–4 minutes. Add carrots, celery, and onions. Cook for another 10 minutes. Add water and wine to cover shells. Season to taste with salt and pepper. Simmer for 1 hour on low.

Strain and reserve liquid in saucepan and keep hot for risotto, or cool and freeze up to three months.

SCORE TIP:

LOBSTER RISOTTO AND LOBSTER STOCK

As mentioned in the beginning of this book, you can easily make stock from the scraps of your vegetables and the bones/shells that you normally throw out. In this recipe for lobster stock, it would behoove you to keep all those precious lobster shells. There is an extraordinary flavor in those leftover shells. Stock is very easy to make and you will taste a world of a difference in your recipes. Once you have cooked and removed all the meat from the shells, set aside in a large bowl until you are ready to make your stock. Shells can be kept in the freezer for up to a month. Heat a large pot with olive oil on high. Add your lobster shells and coat with olive oil. Keep heat on high and cook shells until slightly toasted. Add your veggie scraps to shells and mix together. Add water, wine, salt, and herbs and simmer for 45 minutes to one hour. Place strainer over empty pot and strain lobster stock. Allow to cool. Discard stock content. Place in containers and either freeze up to three months or refrigerate up to one week.

KENNY'S BAKED STUFFED CLAMS (WORLD FAMOUS)

2 dozen cherry stone clams

¼ cup garlic, chopped

½ cup chopped fresh parsley

½ cup white wine

½ cup red pepper, minced

½ cup green pepper, minced

2 tablespoons jalapeño, minced

2 tablespoons pimentos, chopped

1 lemon, squeezed

1 teaspoon lemon zest

1 ½ –2 cups plain bread crumbs

¼ teaspoon cayenne pepper

¼ teaspoon black pepper

1 cup fake lobster-meat sticks, chopped

24 whole clams

Preheat oven to 365 degrees.

In a large stockpot, add all clams and fill with one inch of water. Add garlic, parsley, and wine. Cover with lid and turn heat to high. Wait until water boils and clams open fully, 6–8 minutes, and take pot off heat. Remove clams with tongs, set aside in bowl to cool. Reserve liquid from pot. Pull meat out of clams and put into bowl. Save clam shells.

In food processor, pulse clam meat until chopped. Do not over process clams. Pulse in batches and reserve chopped clam meat in large bowl when finished. Add all remaining ingredients to chopped clam meat and mix until everything is blended. Take reserved liquid and add ¼ cup at a time, not getting mixture too wet. Incorporate until mixture comes together. Add more bread crumbs if mixture is too wet.

Fill each clam shell with 2–3 tablespoons of mixture. Repeat until all clams are stuffed. Bake in oven for 20–22 minutes until top is light golden brown. Serve immediately.

Ex Number Three

Trevor and...

Bruschetta

Cucumber Cups with Mediterranean Salad Filling

Roasted Red Pepper and Caponata Hummus

Barbeque-Potato-Chip-Encrusted Sea Scallops
with Leek, Fennel, and Mushroom Ragout

Stoker Pickled Red Onions and Jalapeños

I met Trevor on one of those infamous dating sites. They advertise, "Meet the love of your life and the man of your dreams." I won't name that site, but I'm sure you can figure it out. Trevor lived in Boston, Massachusetts. We had an instant connection over the phone and talked for hours on end every night. Our initial date was going to be at my girlfriend's house. Really? Was this a good idea? Meeting someone for the first time in front of all of your friends? Well, it sounded like a good idea when I discussed it over cocktails with one of my girlfriends.

"Sure, why not," I said. "That way if he turns out to be a dud, I'll have all my friends there to party with."

I thought I had come up with the best first-date place. My friends, Lisa and Kenny, and I were throwing an end-of-the-summer party on a very hot day in August. Chef Kenny and I spent the whole day cooking in Lisa's tiny kitchen. It was a balmy 95 degrees outside and there was no air conditioning in Lisa's house. The oven temperature was set at 500. I was nervous about the date but still decided to cook the majority of the food. What was I thinking? I must have been high off fresh herbs.

As the party began and all our friends arrived, my nerves were strung out like those of a kid who had eaten a hundred Pixie Stix. Everything was ready to go and my Stoker bruschetta, cucumber cups, garlic herb hummus, and I were making our debuts. The pressure was on because all my girlfriends and I were eager to see what Trevor looked like. He arrived right on time and our chemistry was a match made in heaven—or so I thought. Our conversations were endless and we were finishing each other's sentences by the end of the night. My girlfriends absolutely loved him, and he was cool as a cucumber, given the situation. What a trooper. He definitely was good in my book. As the partying came to an end and the last guests left around 2:00 a.m., Trevor and I continued the evening/morning. We stayed up talking, laughing, and of course making out on my girlfriend's couch. He was a great kisser,

soft, passionate, and in control. As the beautiful sun crested the horizon, we really didn't pay much attention; we both were a little preoccupied with one another. As they say, all good things have to come to an end. It was 7:00 a.m., and Trevor had to leave to be at his sister's place for early morning church service and his nephew's christening. We passionately kissed goodbye in the middle of the street in front of his sporty Range Rover, said our salutations, and he drove off. I walked back to my girlfriend's house in the dress I had on the night before, my hair looking as if a bomb had hit it, no shoes and the biggest smile on my face. I walked into the house and the smell of freshly brewed French vanilla coffee hit my nose. My girlfriend handed me a cup of piping hot coffee and asked me to spill the details. I gave her the lowdown and told her that there would definitely be a second date. So all in all, the party, food, and Trevor were a big hit.

Trevor and I continued to date long distance. The bonus thing about Trevor was that he was a major foodie and loved to talk about food and experiment in the kitchen. He was fluent in his wine knowledge, knew about food, traveled the globe, and spoke several languages. Trevor was a very smart guy, a graduate of the Wharton business school, and on his way to entrepreneurial success. He reminded me of that man in the Dos Equis commercials, "the most interesting man in the world," but did not resemble him in the least bit. A month into our relationship, Trevor invited me to his family's West Island home. We spent all day on his boat and he took me to this private, small island where we had a seaside picnic lunch. The lunch Trevor packed consisted of smoked salmon, caviar, smoked aged cheeses, crackers, exotic fruit, and a nice bottle of chardonnay. I was truly in heaven that day; it couldn't get any better.

We sailed back to the house around dusk and found out that his wacky neighbor had let himself into Trevor's cottage and left a dozen caught-that-day scallops in his fridge. We decided to make dinner with what we had at his beach house, which was very limited. I wanted to spice up the scallops, but all I found was a bag of stale, barbeque potato chips. I crushed them to a fine mixture and encrusted the scallops. And lo and behold, my recipe for barbeque potato-chip-encrusted scallops with sautéed fennel, mushrooms, and pickled red onions was born.

With the barbeque-potato-chip-encrusted scallops and few other accoutrements, we sat on Trevor's porch, which was lit with candles. The ocean was a few yards away, and we had a nice bottle of pinot noir.

The meal was a memorable one; so memorable, I'm still making the dish today. As for Trevor, he wasn't so memorable.

BRUSCHETTA
YIELD: 6–8 SERVINGS

5 vine-ripened tomatoes, diced small

½ red onion, diced small

⅓ cup green onions, chopped

⅓ cup pitted black olives, chopped

1 teaspoon garlic, minced

⅓ cup fresh basil leaves, chopped

DRESSING

¼ cup balsamic vinegar

1 teaspoon mustard

½ teaspoon Italian seasoning

1 tablespoon Parmesan cheese

pinch sugar

¼ cup olive oil

1 baguette cut into ⅓-inch thick slices

olive oil

salt and pepper to taste

In a large bowl, add tomatoes, onions, olives, garlic, and basil. Mix until blended.

In a small bowl, place all dressing ingredients except for olive oil, and mix. Whisk in olive oil slowly until combined. Add to tomato mixture and combine until all ingredients are coated with dressing

Put mixture in fridge for one hour. Cut baguette into 1/3-inch-thick circles. Brush with olive oil and season with salt and pepper. Put in 350-degree oven and bake for 15–20 minutes until light golden brown. Take out of oven and allow to cool. Top each baguette piece with 1–2 tablespoons of the tomato mixture. Garnish with chopped basil.

SCORE TIP:

BRUSCHETTA

Try to find a baguette that has a crunchy, crispy outer crust. Usually French baguettes are your best bet. This will provide the best texture and results for your bruschetta. When the bread is toasted in the oven, the center will remain soft while the outside will have a nice crunchy texture. Use a good olive oil to brush on the top of each bread piece and remember to salt and pepper the bread before it goes into the oven.

Not a fan of olives? You can eliminate the olives in this recipe if you don't care for them. You can replace them with either chopped pimentos or little bites of fresh Parmesan reggiono. The chopped pimentos are found at your local grocery store, usually in a small jar. Just use one jar in this recipe and chop into bite-sized pieces.

CUCUMBER CUPS WITH MEDITERRANEAN SALAD FILLING
YIELD: 8 – 10 SERVINGS

3-4 whole, seedless cucumbers

MEDITERRANEAN FILLING

1 box orzo pasta

⅓ cup balsamic vinegar

½ cup olive oil

⅓ cup capers

¼ cup pimentos, chopped

½ cup green onions, chopped

⅔ cup pitted black olives, chopped

½ red onion, diced small

⅓ cup goat cheese or feta

¼ cup Parmesan cheese

¼ teaspoon ground black pepper

pinch salt

GARNISH

fresh chopped parsley

Cut ends off cucumbers and cut into ½-inch sections. With melon baller, scoop out flesh, leaving bottom of cucumber intact. Place on baking tray. Repeat until all are done. Cover with plastic wrap and place in fridge for several hours.

Make pasta according to package instructions. Drain and rinse in cold water. In bowl, combine vinegar, capers, pimentos, green onions, black olives, and red onions. Add pasta and mix all together. Add olive oil, goat cheese, and Parmesan cheese. Add salt and pepper to taste. Mix until all ingredients are blended.

Take cucumber cups and fill each one with the pasta mixture. Place in fridge until you serve. Garnish with fresh chopped parsley and sea salt.

SCORE TIP:

CUCUMBER CUPS WITH MEDITERRANEAN SALAD FILLING

PASTA: This recipe calls for orzo pasta, which looks like rice grains. It is usually found in the pasta aisle at your local grocery store. If you cannot find this type of pasta, you can replace it with very small pasta shaped like tiny shells: ditalini (little thimble-shaped pasta) and pastina (star-shaped pasta).

ROASTED RED PEPPER AND CAPONATA HUMMUS

YIELD: 4–6 SERVINGS

1 small can caponata (found in the Italian section of your local grocery store)

⅓ cup roasted red peppers, drained and chopped

2 medium whole garlic cloves, halved

1 tablespoon capers

2 (15 oz) cans chick peas, drained

¼ teaspoon red pepper flakes

½–¾ cup olive oil

salt and pepper

2 tablespoons fresh chives, chopped

Blend everything except olive oil in food processor. Blend until all ingredients are combined. Add oil slowly while machine is running. Blend until smooth. Season with salt and pepper.

Refrigerate for several hours before serving. Serve with pita chips or crackers.

SCORE TIP:

ROASTED RED PEPPER AND CAPONATA HUMMUS

Caponata is a Sicilian sweet and sour eggplant dish, usually made with eggplant, tomatoes, olives, capers, celery, and good vinegar. Sicilian caponata is similar to southern French ratatouille. It is usually a side dish or appetizer and is served at room temperature. It's a very easy appetizer to make for your friends and family. Always use the freshest, firmest eggplant and tomatoes you can find. Cooking the ingredients separately in the same pan, then mixing them afterwards, improves the quality of the caponata. In this recipe, since time is of the essence, I use canned caponata found in the Italian section of your local grocery store.

barbeque-potato-chip-encrusted sea scallops with leek, fennel, and mushroom ragout

BARBEQUE-POTATO-CHIP-ENCRUSTED SEA SCALLOPS WITH LEEK, FENNEL, AND MUSHROOM RAGOUT

YIELD: 4 SERVINGS

12 sea scallops

½ cup flour

2 eggs, beaten

1 tablespoon water

2 cups crushed barbeque thin potato chips

salt and pepper

2 tablespoons olive oil

½ teaspoon chopped fresh garlic

2 tablespoons red onion, chopped

2 fennel bulbs, cores removed, thinly sliced

2 leeks, top and bottom stems removed, white part only, thinly sliced

2 cups button mushrooms, stems removed, thinly sliced

⅓ cup chicken broth

¼ cup balsamic vinegar

2 tablespoons grated Parmesan

Take three small bowls and add flour to one, a beaten egg combined with water to the second, and crushed chips to the third.

Salt and pepper both sides of a scallop. Dip in flour mixture first and shake off excess. Dip in egg mixture. Then coat generously with crushed chips. Repeat until all scallops are coated. Set aside on plate and put in freezer for 30 minutes.

In large sauté pan, heat olive oil on medium-high. Add garlic and onions. Sauté for a few minutes until onions are soft. Add fennel and leeks. Sauté for 10 minutes. Add mushrooms. Cook for 6–7 minutes. Add chicken broth and vinegar. Cook until all ingredients are soft and liquid is almost gone. Add Parmesan to finish. Season with salt and pepper to taste.

In another sauté pan, heat olive oil on high until pan is very hot. Sauté scallops for 2–3 minutes per side. Sauté longer for a more well-done consistency. Serve over fennel mixture.

BARBEQUE-POTATO-CHIP-ENCRUSTED SEA SCALLOPS WITH LEEK, FENNEL, AND MUSHROOM RAGOUT

The best kind of potato chip to use in this recipe is the very thin, crispy kind. If you're not a fan of barbeque, you can use any flavored potato chip. My second favorite flavor for this recipe is salt and vinegar. The tangy vinegar powder on the chips really makes the sea scallops pop and blends the flavors of the leek, fennel, and mushroom ragout. If flavored chips are not your thing, then a plain, salted, thin potato chip will also work.

FENNEL: If you honestly don't know what fennel is, have no fear. I am here to enlighten your minds and give you a brief overview of this wonderful vegetable. Fennel has a white or pale green bulb and tough, green stalks with feathery fronds. Usually the bulb is eaten and the fronds can be used for garnish. Fennel has a very distinct flavor of anise and mild licorice with the texture of celery. The bulb is made of overlapping layers, almost like a cabbage. Fennel's subtle flavor works just fine on its own but does wonders when combined with other foods. Pairing fennel with seafood, especially scallops, really brings out the freshness of the seafood and makes the seafood flavors more pronounced. A fennel salad with oranges, red onions, and dill, paired with a grilled, rare tuna steak, takes the flavor of the tuna to a whole new level.

STOKER PICKLED RED ONIONS AND JALAPEÑOS

2 medium-sized red onions, sliced thin

2 large jalapeños, halved, seeds removed, and cut into thin strips

2 ½ cups orange juice

½ cup apple cider vinegar

1 tablespoon kosher salt

½ teaspoon cracked pepper

¼ teaspoon red pepper flakes

In medium bowl, add orange juice, vinegar, salt, pepper, and red pepper flakes. Mix together. Add onions and jalapeños. Refrigerate for 4–6 hours. Marinate overnight for a more intense, pickled flavor.

Ex Number Four

Jimmy and...

Lobster Panzanella Salad

Barbeque Lobster Quesadilla

Looking Good and Feeling Good Martini

Fried Plantains Topped with Chipotle-Cinnamon Pulled Pork
and Jicama Salsa

Parmesan Baskets Filled with Caesar Salad and Croutons

Chayote Salsa

Cinnamon-Chipotle-Barbeque Chicken Wings
and Yogurt-Cucumber Sauce

I was in Charlotte, North Carolina, for a huge food and wine festival sponsored by my company. I was there to perform my very first chef demo. I felt every feel-good emotion underneath the sun: on cloud nine, living the life, my shining moment, yell at the top of your lungs—you get the idea, right? I couldn't believe I had been given the chance to do what I had always dreamed about: prepare amazing food, teach, talk, and entertain a live audience—finally, my lucky break. In my own silly, off-the-wall thinking, I was on my way to celebrity chef stardom.

As the week progressed, I worked fourteen/fifteen-hour days, prepping and helping out with the main stage productions on top of getting ready for my own chef demo. The food and wine festival was the food event of the year for the folks of North Carolina. It was a three-day festival, loaded with extremely talented chefs, celebrity chefs, barbeque cook-offs, and every food fair vendor imaginable. Being new to the company, I didn't really know a lot of people, but I felt reassured because my mom and friend, Lisa, were there to support me. When the day of my demonstration came, I arrived at 5:00 a.m. to a deserted, pin-drop-quiet kitchen that normally housed 200–300 chefs a day and looked like Grand Central station at rush hour. The calm and silence of the kitchen allowed me to focus and prepare for my demo. Later that morning, I found out that two people had been assigned to assist me during my demo: Jimmy and Tiffany. Jimmy was an attractive, funny, tattoo-laden, sly guy, who exuded an air of confidence. We had instant chemistry and I was really digging his sense of humor. It made him irresistible. As the two worked hard to help me get ready, I prepped them on my plans for the demo. My menu was lobster stock, lobster panzanella salad, lobster quesadilla, and looking good and feeling-good martini.

Five minutes before showtime, my heart pounded. Jimmy tried to calm my nerves by performing his own comedy routine to make me laugh. A large, hungry crowd gathered outside my stage area, and I knew this was my time to shine. The stage director came over and wired my microphone, fitted the ear piece, positioned my headset, and I was ready to go. Two deep breaths and I instantly went into my zone. I was born to do this. I was in my element on stage. My demo was a success and Jimmy was a great assistant throughout the whole thing. We both interacted with the crowd so well that it felt like the Chef Jenn Show, with a little splash of Jimmy.

After the food and wine festival, I couldn't stop thinking about Jimmy. I decided to e-mail him, knowing that he wasn't remotely close to where I lived. We instantly sparked a great connection. The only downside was that Jimmy was in Boston and I was in Connecticut. Despite the distance, Jimmy drove down almost every weekend to see me.

Dating another chef was a first for me. There was a hint of competitiveness between us when we cooked together, which we did a few times, and I think those few times were enough because they would always end in an argument. But in the end, it was great to learn culinary techniques from a different point of view and sometimes I actually learned a thing or two from him. I just wasn't about to tell him that.

As we dated for a few months, I started to see that Jimmy and I weren't compatible. I was falling out of love with Jimmy. He had so much drama in his life that I was overwhelmed and wanted out. And here's the kicker: he was still married. Yes, still married. His divorce was not official. So, that was a huge enough red flag for me to call it quits with Jimmy.

Before I could call it quits with Mr. Jimmy, he was scheduled to help me cater my girlfriend's Valentine's Day party in Baltimore, Maryland. Since my girlfriend Rachael had designed all my logos and basically branded my newly launched personal chef business, we took it out in trade: I cooked all the food for her huge V-Day bash.

Some of the recipes I created for her party included Parmesan baskets filled with Caesar salads, chayote salsa, cinnamon-chipotle-barbeque chicken wings, and fried plantains topped with cinnamon-chipotle pulled pork and jicama salsa. The night was stressful because the tension between Jimmy and I was intense, just like two raging bulls about to stampede through a crowd of people. Even before the party started, Jimmy didn't understand that I was the chef in charge and he didn't like my barking orders. Being a guy, I guess he didn't like being told to what to do by a woman. Overall, this was my gig and he was the sous chef. An explosive argument erupted thirty minutes before the party started and Rachael came running into the kitchen to break it up. Jimmy stormed out of the kitchen, threw the front door open, and walked briskly down the street. I was left to do it all myself. Rachael jumped in to help me garnish and finish off all the food. We both were shuttling out the food when the first ten guests arrived. Lo and behold, my food got rave reviews from the guests and that made all my stress go away. Jimmy returned thirty minutes later. We didn't know where he'd gone, but I'm sure the Baltimore cold kept him from going too far, and of course, the yummy martinis at the end of the evening helped melt the pain away—as they always do.

LOBSTER PANZANELLA SALAD
YIELD: 4–6 SERVINGS

4 large, vine-ripened tomatoes, medium diced

1 small cucumber, with skins on, medium diced

1 small red onion, diced small

⅓ cup fresh basil leaves, roughly chopped

½ cup avocado, diced small

2 ½ cups toasted bread, hard crusted, cut into bite-sized pieces

⅓ cup green onions, roughly chopped

1 cup cooked lobster meat, chopped

DRESSING

¼ cup balsamic vinegar

2 tablespoons red wine vinegar

1 teaspoon yellow mustard

2 tablespoons milk

½ teaspoon each dried oregano and dried basil

½ teaspoon sugar

pinch black pepper

¼ teaspoon each of salt and red pepper flakes

⅓ cup olive oil

In medium bowl, combine all ingredients except for dressing. Set aside.

For dressing: in small bowl, add all ingredients except for oil. Whisk together. Drizzle oil onto ingredients slowly while whisking back and forth. Whisk dressing until all ingredients are combined. Pour over bread mixture and toss to combine until all ingredients are coated with the dressing. Season with salt and pepper to taste, if necessary. Serve immediately.

SCORE TIP:

LOBSTER PANZANELLA SALAD

Why do you use milk in vinaigrette? Milk or any other cream-like ingredient used in vinaigrette helps reduce the acidity and gives the vinaigrette a smooth taste. In this recipe, I only use a few tablespoons of regular milk. When adding milk or cream to vinaigrette, you only need a small amount because you don't want to dilute the vinaigrette or make it too creamy. A little bit of cream/milk goes a long way.

If your budget is limited or you don't care for lobster, here are some suggestions for substitutes: cooked shrimp, jumbo lump crab meat, chopped pepperoni, prosciutto, or salami.

BARBEQUE LOBSTER QUESADILLA

YIELD: 4 SERVINGS

1 ½ cups cooked lobster meat, chopped

1 can black beans, drained

½ cup corn

½ cup barbeque sauce

⅓ cup red onion, diced small

¼ cup green onion, chopped

¼ cup fresh cilantro, roughly chopped

¼ teaspoon dried coriander, ground

½ teaspoon cumin

1 teaspoon Worcestershire sauce

1 teaspoon hot sauce

1 lime, juiced

salt and pepper

1 cup queso fresco crumbled, or shredded mozzarella cheese

large flour tortillas, 12-inch

Combine all ingredients in bowl except tortillas. Mix until all ingredients are incorporated.

In large sauté pan on high heat, place 2 tablespoons of olive oil. Place tortilla in skillet, put ½-⅔ cup of lobster mixture on one side of tortilla. Fold over, slightly press down. Cook until golden brown on one side, then flip and brown the other side. Lobster mixture should be hot throughout and cheese should be melted. Add more cheese if desired. Take off heat, place on cutting board, and cut into triangles. Serve with salsa and sour cream.

SCORE TIP:

BARBEQUE LOBSTER QUESADILLA

As I discussed in the previous tip on lobsters, even though warm-water lobsters are not the best lobsters to use for their flavor properties compared to their cold-water counterparts, in this recipe I highly recommend using the cheaper, warm-water lobsters. The reason behind my madness is that so many flavors/ingredients are used in this recipe that the lobster meat is not the main focus of the dish. If the lobster were the main focus, you would want to use a cold-water lobster.

What is queso fresco? A staple item in Mexican cuisine, queso fresco is fresh cheese. It is very mild, tangy, and slightly salty and is a great replacement for mozzarella cheese. Despite its salty taste, queso fresco is surprisingly low in sodium and fat. Hispanic cheeses are different from American and European cheeses. They look, cook, and taste very different. A lot of Hispanic cheeses rarely melt. When these fresh cheeses become warm and soft, they do not lose their shape or run all over the plate in the cooking process. This characteristic is essential in many Hispanic dishes, which is good to keep in mind if you are cooking any kind of dish for which you want the cheese to stay intact but still give the dish a creamy, gooey texture.

champagne-sorbet cocktail

looking good and feeling good martini

LOOKING GOOD AND FEELING GOOD MARTINI

1 cup ice

2 shots vodka (Have a gluten allergy? Use potato vodka.)

¼ cup acai juice

¼ cup cranberry juice

⅓ cup freshly squeezed blood orange juice (or regular orange juice)

¼ cup sugar

2 tablespoons honey

In cocktail shaker, add all ingredients except sugar and honey. Take two small plates. On one plate place honey and on the other plate place sugar in a pile. Coat rim of martini glass with honey. Coat honeyed rim with sugar. In cocktail shaker, shake vigorously for 20 seconds and pour in martini glass.

SCORE TIP:

LOOKING GOOD AND FEELING GOOD MARTINI

What is vodka made from? Good question, right? Never really thought about that, right? You just know that it makes you feel good. Vodka is made through the process of distillation of a fermented substance, often potatoes, rye, or wheat grain. Most vodka was traditionally made from potatoes and corn, but in recent years, most high-quality brands of vodka have been distilled from cereal grains. The potatoes and grains are heated until the starch is released and converted to sugar. Then this substance, called a mash, is fermented and heated to a high temperature to allow distillation to occur. Water is added at the end of the distillation process to decrease the alcohol content, and then the vodka is ready to be bottled and sold. With the growing number of food allergies today, gluten-free diets are on the rise. If you love your vodka as much as I do and can't have any type of wheat/gluten-based products, your best bet is to drink potato-based vodka. There a many high-quality potato-vodka brands on the market today. What comes to mind—and is one of my favorites—is the Tito's brand. So, you still will look good and feel good when drinking this martini.

Champagne-Sorbet Cocktail: For this beverage concoction of mine, the best type of champagne to use is semisweet. It balances out the sweetness of the sorbet and makes a nice, smooth cocktail. The best sorbet flavors to use are raspberry, mango and/or strawberry. You don't want to use really acidic sorbet flavors such as lemon, lime, or pineapple.

FRIED PLANTAINS TOPPED WITH CHIPOTLE-CINNAMON PULLED PORK AND JICAMA SALSA

YIELD: 6–8 SERVINGS

4-6 plantains cut into ½-inch circles

canola oil for frying

BRINE FOR PORK

3-4 pound pork shoulder

¾ gallon water

⅓ cup salt

½ cup sugar

1 teaspoon cinnamon

⅓ cup Worcestershire sauce

2 dried chipotle peppers (or 2 teaspoons dry chipotle powder)

1 teaspoon whole peppercorns

2 tablespoons olive oil

BRAISE LIQUID

1 quart chicken stock

½ cup ketchup

2 tablespoons Worcestershire sauce

¼ teaspoon cinnamon

salt and pepper

JICAMA SALSA

1 large jicama, peeled and diced small

½ cup chopped red peppers

1 cup pineapple tidbits

½ red onion, diced small

⅓ cup fresh cilantro, chopped

1 tablespoon fresh parsley, chopped

2 tablespoons apple cider vinegar

2 tablespoons olive oil

salt and pepper

To make the brine: place all brine ingredients in large container and mix well. Place pork in brine solution, cover, and put into fridge for 12–24 hours.

Remove pork from brine and pat dry. Discard brine solution. In medium roasting pan, place all braising liquid ingredients. Mix together thoroughly. Place pork in roasting pan, cover with foil, and put into oven for 4–6 hours at 300 degrees. When pork is done, it should easily shred with a fork.

To make jicama salsa: in medium bowl, combine all ingredients and mix. Set aside in fridge.

To make plantains: in a large deep skillet heat, 1 ½ inches of oil to 375 degrees. Peel plantains and slice into ¼ inch circles. Smash with meat mallet until flat. Fry 4–6 plantains at a time until golden brown. Drain on paper towel and season with salt and pepper. Repeat. Keep fried plantains warm in a low-heat oven.

Once pork is done and fork tender, remove from roasting pan. Place roasting pan on stove and bring liquid to a rolling boil. Reduce sauce by half. Shred pork and place back in sauce. Combine.

Take plantain and spoon 1 tablespoon of pork mixture on top. Top with jicama salsa. Serve.

SCORE TIP:

FRIED PLANTAINS TOPPED WITH CHIPOTLE-CINNAMON PULLED PORK AND JICAMA SALSA

It would be a major sin to throw out the juices created from your pulled pork. These juices are the heart and soul of the effort you took to cook this delicious dish. So, now that you have this delicious pulled pork, what are you going to do with the juice? The best thing to do is to save it and add it to your future creations. Take an empty ice cube tray and fill ¾ of each slot with the cooled pork juice. Freeze cubes until they are solid, remove from mold, and save in a Ziploc bag in your freezer for up to two months. You can add the pork juice cube to your others sauces, soups, and stews. This will take all your dishes to a whole new level.

parmesan baskets filled with caesar salad and croutons

PARMESAN BASKETS FILLED WITH CAESAR SALAD AND CROUTONS

1½-2 pounds shaved or shredded Parmesan cheese

nonstick cooking spray

Preheat oven to 350 degrees.

Spray a baking sheet lightly with a nonstick spray. Take ¼ cup shaved or shredded Parmesan cheese and spread evenly in individual mounds on the baking sheet. Space evenly. Bake for 12–14 minutes until light golden brown. Take out of oven and cool for 1 minute. Take small coffee cups and turn upside down, lay Parmesan sheet over cup and allow to dry. Work fast and this will form the basket. Repeat until all Parmesan baskets are molded. Allow to cool 10–15 minute on cups.

PARMESAN BASKETS FILLED WITH CAESAR SALAD AND CROUTONS

If you looked at the photo on the page opposite the Parmesan basket recipe, and you thought, "Hell no, I can't do that," well, I'm about to change your mind. These little baskets may look intimidating to make, but they are very simple to execute. All you need is: baking sheets, cooking spray, small coffee cups, a spatula, and a container for storage.

The best type of Parmesan cheese to use when making your Parmesan baskets is shredded. I have tested these baskets out and the powdered Parmesan cheese really doesn't form that well when it's in the oven. It tends to fall apart and not hold its shape. The shredded Parmesan works the best for these baskets.

When baking the Parmesan circles, the best thing to use on the baking sheet to help prevent them from sticking is a nonstick cooking spray. A light coating on the baking sheet will help the Parmesan circles lift off very easily. When the Parmesan circles are finished baking, take out of oven and allow to rest for 30 seconds before laying over coffee mugs. Make sure you allow them to cool and completely harden before removing them from mugs.

Not up on making your own croutons or just don't have the time? Buy them at the store. Try to find the smallest size possible.

CAESAR SALAD

2 heads romaine lettuce, ends removed, chopped into small pieces

1 teaspoon garlic, minced

1 egg*

½ teaspoon anchovy paste

1 tablespoon lemon juice

¼ cup apple cider vinegar

2 teaspoons Dijon mustard

½ teaspoon Worcestershire sauce

4-5 drops hot sauce

2 tablespoons Parmesan cheese

½ cup of oil

*Consuming raw or undercooked meats, poultry, shellfish, and eggs may increase your risk of food-borne illness.

To make dressing: in blender, place all ingredients except oil. Blend on low setting until all ingredients are incorporated. Drizzle oil while blender is on. Mix dressing with romaine lettuce. Season with salt and pepper. Add Caesar salad to Parmesan bowl. Top with croutons.

CROUTONS

2 cups hard, crusty bread, cut into very small pieces

oil for frying, canola or vegetable

Heat 1/4 inch oil in small frying pan until very hot. Add bread cubes and fry until golden brown. Drain on paper towel. Season with salt and pepper.

CHAYOTE SALSA

2 chayote squashes, boiled, shocked, peeled, and diced small

1 red pepper, seeds and white pith removed, diced small

1 yellow pepper, seeds and white pith removed, diced small

⅓ cup green onion, chopped

¼ cup fresh cilantro, chopped

1 jalapeño, white pith and seeds removed, chopped into small pieces

½ red onion, diced small

¼ cup apple cider vinegar

½ teaspoon hot sauce

2 tablespoons olive oil

salt and pepper to taste

To cook chayote: in medium saucepan, bring salted water to a boil. Add whole chayote and cook for 6–8 minutes. Remove from water and shock in a bowl of ice water to stop the cooking process. Leave in ice water for 2–3 minutes. Drain in strainer, peel off skins, and cut into small dice.

Add all ingredients to large bowl. Mix together. Season with salt and pepper to taste. Refrigerate for 2 hours. Serve with pita or tortilla chips.

SCORE TIP:

CHAYOTE SALSA (PRONOUNCED CHAH-YOH-TEH)

If you have never seen a chayote squash, it looks like an old man's mouth without any teeth. Kind of an odd comparison, but this is the first thing that comes to mind when I see this vegetable. Chayote squashes are now fairly popular and found in local grocery stores. They can be eaten raw and used in salsas as in this recipe, but they are best when you cook them slightly. Since they already have a mild flavor, cooking them slightly will bring out more of their natural flavor. When buying them, you should look for the chayotes to be light green in color, firm, smooth skinned, and unwrinkled. When cooking chayotes, it's best to boil, bake, or sauté. There is a small, soft seed in the center that is edible, but some choose to remove the seed. In this recipe, I remove the seed.

If you can't find chayotes in your local grocery store, you can replace them with yellow squash. The best way to cook the yellow squash is to cut them into bite-sized pieces and sauté them with some olive oil until slightly soft. Allow to cool before you add to the salsa ingredients.

CINNAMON-CHIPOTLE-BARBEQUE CHICKEN WINGS AND YOGURT-CUCUMBER SAUCE

YIELD: 6–8 SERVINGS

6–8 lb. frozen chicken wings

3 ½ cups ketchup

¼ cup (can) chipotles in adobe sauce, chopped

½ teaspoon cinnamon

2 tablespoons honey

1 cup beef broth

1 tablespoon Worcestershire sauce

Thaw wings.

Preheat oven to 425 degrees.

In medium saucepan, mix all ingredients together. Cook on medium heat for 20–25 minutes. Take off heat and allow to cool. In large bowl, add wings. Pour half of sauce mixture over wings and incorporate until all wings are coated. Put in fridge for 4–6 hours. Marinate overnight for a more intense flavor.

Lay out on baking sheet, side by side. Put in oven for 25 minutes. After 25 minutes, take out and brush remaining sauce over wings. Put back in oven for another 22–25 minutes, or until chicken is completely cooked. Serve with yogurt-cucumber sauce.

SCORE TIP:

CINNAMON-CHIPOTLE-BARBEQUE CHICKEN WINGS

Have a dairy allergy or intolerance? Replace the plain yogurt with a plain soy yogurt. You will get the same taste and flavor in this sauce recipe without the dairy. Soy yogurt can be found at any natural food store or your nearest Whole Foods store. The cucumbers used in this recipe act as a palate cooler. Since the chipotle peppers are spicy, the cucumber and yogurt combination helps cool things down.

YOGURT-CUCUMBER SAUCE

1 ½ cups plain yogurt

½ cup cucumber, skins removed, finely chopped

1 teaspoon ground cumin

1 teaspoon chili powder

1 teaspoon lemon juice

salt/pepper to taste

Peel cucumber and finely chop. Put chopped cucumbers in strainer over bowl and allow water to drain from cucumbers. Let sit in strainer for 30 minutes. Add strained cucumbers, ground cumin, chili powder, and lemon juice to yogurt. Incorporate until all is blended together. Season to taste with salt and pepper.

Ex Number Five

Brad and...

Grilled Lamb with Asian Pesto, Thai Cabbage Slaw, and Coconut-Lemon Sauce

Moroccan-Caribbean Chicken Stew with Cilantro-Jasmine Rice

Moroccan-Mexican Chicken Stew over Basmati Rice

Japanese Citrus Salmon with Soba Noodles and Sautéed Garlic Bok Choy

Tuscan-Style Rigatoni with Braised Tomatoes, Spinach, and Italian Sausage in Light Tomato-Broth Sauce

When Brad tasted my food for the first time, I was preparing for a chef demo at a Kiwanis' conference, and I wanted to test out my food before I actually performed my demo. So I had invited a few friends over to my humble little abode and Brad was one of my guests. Now at this point, we only had been dating for a few weeks. The main dish I was testing out on all my guinea pigs was the grilled lamb with an Asian pesto sauce and spicy Thai cabbage slaw with coconut sauce.

Let me set the scene for this particular gem of a guy. Brad: good looking, 6-foot-2, very lean, Lance Armstrong-wanna-be, trust-fund baby, early 40s, no real job his whole life, ski bum, furniture king, and wacky-weed enjoyer from time to time.

I met Brad at a friend of a friend's house party on a beautiful, crisp, fall night. She introduced us and we hit it off immediately.

For our first date, Brad took me to a quaint, Connecticut restaurant. It was a small, cottage restaurant in the woods in a picturesque Norman Rockwell town. The food was so-so, but I was more into the company I was with. Talk about basic first-date things: What do you do? Where do you live? Blah, blah, blah...Brad worked at his brother's small financial company as "errand boy"—translation: going door to door and picking up his brother's clients' monthly financial statements. By the end of the night we were finishing each other's sentences and we were the last ones in the restaurant. The impatient server, who wanted us to leave, brought the check over, set it down right in front of Brad, and stormed off. To be polite on first dates I always ask, "Do you need a contribution?" But any girl knows that a true gentleman who asks you out on a date would always decline your offer and pay the check, right? Well, not Brad. He asked me how much of a contribution I could pay toward the check. Yes, ladies and gentlemen, close your gaping mouths. It gets better.

I don't know if it was the grilled lamb dish that I made for Brad, or if it was the hot, steamy, passionate night of sex we had, but after that night, I started creating some amazing dishes for us: Japanese citrus salmon with soba noodles and sautéed garlic bok choy; Moroccan-Mexican chicken stew over basmati rice; and Tuscan-style rigatoni with braised tomatoes, spinach, and Italian sausage in a light tomato-broth sauce. In every recipe, you can taste the passion and love in each bite. Making these recipes, you will definitely score in the end.

Toward the end of the rocky, roller coaster relationship, I decided that I wanted to have a thirty-third birthday party and celebrate in style with all my friends. Brad and I decided to host the party at his parents' mansion in Connecticut. We invited our crazy friends and he invited some of his family who lived nearby. The bar was well stocked with every type of liquor imaginable and we even had a do-it-yourself Mojito bar with every type of accoutrement known to man. I think all the men at the party really enjoyed hanging around the Mojito bar because my girlfriend with the big boobs ended up feverishly muddling everyone's Mojito drinks. Her low-cut dress and boobs bouncing around as if a she were on a trampoline, was like a mini-peep show for them. Not only did the abundance of liquor overwhelm the subdued crowd, the food was out of this world as well. What do you expect when you invite your chef friends and Brad's mom made her stellar Italian dishes? With marinated cold shrimp with fresh basil and tomatoes, gourmet deviled eggs with jalapeño topping, stuffed endive leaves with prosciutto and pancetta, gourmet sub sandwiches, homemade biscotti, and eggplant canapés, the gourmet feast was endless.

The nonpartying, older folks had gone home by midnight and everyone who remained filled up on petro shots and skinny-bitch beverages (diet coke and vanilla vodka). By 3:00 a.m. Brad's parents were fast asleep and Christina, Jerry, Brad, Jake, and I were in the kitchen acting like drunken fools. Then smart, intelligent Brad whipped out a joint, lit it up like Bob Marley sitting around a campfire, and he and Jake puffed away to happy land. His parents were thirty feet away in their bedroom, not knowing the shenanigans that were going on. My two cronies and I ignored the drug fest and continued down our road to never-never land; we were happy in our own little world.

Our ADD levels were rapidly going up, and all of a sudden Jerry stripped to his Superman skivvies, attempted a gymnastics cartwheel, hit the wall, and landed flat on the floor. He started hugging the wall, and then he lay there like a frightened possum. As we all broke into laughter, we heard footsteps coming toward the kitchen. Brad's mom appeared in the doorway in her robe and house slippers. She looked confused, upset, and ready to scream at all of us. The whole room smelled like pot, and Jerry was still lying on the floor in his superhero skivvies, not moving. She looked at us, and Jerry, and asked, "Is he okay?"

Mortified, we could only nod our heads.

"Can you all please keep it down?" she said. "And, Bradley, can I talk to you in private?"

So, the forty-one-year-old Bradley marched off down the hallway with his head lowered to be scolded by his mommy. Lesson learned ladies: when a guy asks you out on a first date and you have to pay half of the check, you might find yourself in a relationship like this.

grilled lamb with asian pesto, thai cabbage slaw, and coconut lemon sauce

GRILLED LAMB WITH ASIAN PESTO, THAI CABBAGE SLAW, AND COCONUT-LEMON SAUCE

YIELD: 4 SERVINGS

4 (5-6oz) lean lamb filets

Salt and pepper

Olive oil

ASIAN PESTO

1- ⅓ cups basil leaves

½ cup of mint leaves

⅓ cup fresh cilantro, stems removed

1 tablespoon coriander seed

1 cup unsalted peanuts

1 tablespoon fresh ginger, chopped

1 teaspoon fresh garlic, chopped

1 tablespoon lemon juice

½ – ¾ cup light olive oil

Salt and pepper

THAI CHILI CABBAGE SLAW

4 cups of green cabbage, sliced thin

2 cups of purple cabbage, sliced thin

¾ cup shredded carrots

⅓ cup of rice vinegar

1 – 2 teaspoons Thai chili sauce (depends on your heat level)

½ tablespoon lemon juice

1 teaspoon sugar

Salt and pepper

1 tablespoon neutral oil (vegetable oil)

Salt and pepper

COCONUT SAUCE

1 can regular coconut milk

½ tablespoon lemon juice

1 tablespoon rice vinegar

2 teaspoons honey

Salt/pepper

GARNISHES

Thin toasted bagel slice and fresh chives or rosemary sprigs

Asian Pesto: In food processor, add all ingredients except for olive oil. Blend all ingredients together, drizzle in olive oil slowly as food processor or blender is on. Blend until smooth. If pesto is too thick, add more oil.

Coconut Sauce: In small sauce pan, add all ingredients and bring to boil. Mix well until everything is incorporated. Lower heat to a simmer and cook for 20 minutes. Set aside and allow to cool.

Thai Chili Cabbage Slaw: In large bowl, add carrots and green and purple cabbage. Toss together. In small bowl, add the remainder of ingredients. Mix together until all ingredients are incorporated. Pour wet mixture over cabbage. Toss together until all cabbage is coated. Set aside in fridge.

Lamb: Coat each lamb filet with olive oil, salt, and pepper, on both sides. Heat grill to 375 or sauté pan with olive oil on high heat. Grill or sear lamb until desired consistency.

Allow to rest. Slice into very thin strips.

On plate, take ¾ cup of slaw and put in middle. Lay strips of the lamb 4–5 on top of the slaw, like a fan. Drizzle Asian pesto over lamb. Take bagel slice and lay on side of slaw, with chives or rosemary sprigs strung through the middle. Drizzle dish with coconut sauce.

moroccan-caribbean chicken stew with cilantro-jasmine rice

MOROCCAN-CARIBBEAN CHICKEN STEW WITH CILANTRO-JASMINE RICE

YIELD: 4–6 SERVINGS

1 lb. chicken breast, boneless, skinless, cubed

¼ cup olive oil

2 teaspoons jerk seasoning

⅛ teaspoon ground clove

¼ cup molasses

¼ teaspoon black pepper

2 tablespoons olive oil

1 teaspoon garlic, chopped

⅓ cup green onions, chopped

1 small butternut squash, peeled, seeds removed, medium diced

2 yellow squashes, top and bottom removed, medium diced

1 medium red pepper, diced small

1 teaspoon ground cumin

1 teaspoon fennel seeds

½ teaspoon red pepper flakes

⅔ cup chicken stock

1 (15 oz.) can stewed tomatoes

2 tablespoons tomato paste

1 teaspoon lemon juice

salt and pepper

jasmine rice, cooked

GARNISH

fresh cilantro, chopped

Place chicken in a bowl and add oil, jerk seasoning, cloves, molasses, salt, and pepper. Incorporate until chicken is coated and all ingredients are blended. Set aside in fridge for one hour.

In large sauté pan, heat 2 tablespoons of olive oil on medium-high. Add garlic and green onions. Cook for 2–3 minutes. Reduce heat to medium and add chicken mixture. Cook for 9–10 minutes. Add butternut squash, yellow squash, and pepper. Cook for 10–12 minutes. Add spices. Blend together. Add chicken stock, tomatoes, tomato paste, and lemon juice. Mix together, cover with lid, and cook for 20–22 minutes on medium-low heat until vegetables are al dente and sauce thickens. Stir often. Season with salt and pepper.

Cook rice according to package instructions. Serve over rice. Garnish with fresh cilantro.

SCORE TIP:

MOROCCAN-CARIBBEAN CHICKEN STEW WITH CILANTRO-JASMINE RICE

Let's talk molasses. What is the thick, black, sticky substance? It's a byproduct of the processing of sugar cane and beet sugar. It's not as sweet as maple syrup or pure honey, but its distinctive bite sets it above the rest. Brown sugar is made with molasses, which makes it stronger in flavor than regular sugar.

Molasses has somewhat more nutritional value than regular white sugar. Molasses is treated with sulfur as the sugars are being processed and this results in its fortification with iron, calcium, and magnesium.

If you don't have molasses on hand, you can substitute brown sugar.

MOROCCAN-MEXICAN CHICKEN STEW OVER BASMATI RICE

YIELD: 4 SERVINGS

2 tablespoons olive oil

1 large green pepper, medium diced

½ red onion, diced small

1 teaspoon garlic, chopped

1 lb. chicken breasts, boneless, skinless, cubed

salt and pepper

1 teaspoon ground cumin

½ teaspoon chili powder

¼ teaspoon ground black pepper

2 teaspoons curry powder

1 large tomato, medium diced

¼ cup roasted red peppers, chopped

⅓ cup hot banana peppers, chopped

½ cup chicken stock

1 can stew tomatoes

1 tablespoon tomato paste

salt to taste

1 lime, juiced

¼ cup fresh cilantro, torn

cooked basmati rice

Cook basmati rice according to package instructions. Set aside and keep warm.

In medium stockpot, add olive oil and heat on medium-high. Add green pepper, onion, and garlic. Sauté for 5–6 minutes. Add chicken and all spices. Cook for 10–12 minutes. Add tomatoes, roasted red peppers, and banana peppers. Lower heat to medium. Continue to cook for another 5 minutes. Add chicken stock, stewed tomatoes, and tomato paste and incorporate with other ingredients. Simmer for 20–25 minutes on low heat, stirring occasionally. Turn off heat and add lime juice and fresh cilantro. Serve over basmati rice.

JAPANESE CITRUS SALMON WITH SOBA NOODLES AND SAUTÉED GARLIC BOK CHOY

YIELD: 4 SERVINGS

4 salmon fillets, with skin

1 tablespoon lemon zest

1 tablespoon fresh rosemary

1 ¼ teaspoon sea salt

¼ teaspoon ground black pepper

CITRUS SAUCE

1 - ½ cups of orange juice

2 tablespoons soy sauce

½–1 teaspoon chili paste (depending on your preferred level of heat)

1 tablespoon fresh ginger, minced

2 tablespoons mango puree or juice

BROTH

2 cups chicken stock

3 tablespoons mango puree or juice

1 tablespoon soy sauce

1 tablespoon rice wine vinegar

1 teaspoon fresh ginger, minced

½ lemon, juiced

SAUTÉ

2 tablespoons olive oil

1 teaspoon garlic, chopped

¼ cup green onion, chopped

4 baby bok choys, chopped

Japanese rice noodles

GARNISH

fresh chopped chives (optional)

Preheat oven to 350 degrees.

In small bowl, place lemon zest, rosemary, sea salt, and black pepper. Blend together. Take salmon fillets and evenly season salmon with spice mixture. Set aside in fridge for 30 minutes.

To make broth: add all ingredients to saucepan, heat to boil, and then reduce to slow simmer for 30 minutes. Cover with lid.

To make citrus sauce: in bowl, stir all ingredients to combine and set aside.

Cook noodles according to package instructions and keep warm.

Heat olive oil in medium sauté pan on high until very hot. Add salmon fillets, skin side down. Cook for 3–4 minutes. Do not flip. Put whole pan in oven to finish cooking. Cook for another 4–8 minutes in oven or until desired doneness. Take fish out of pan and set aside. Heat pan on stove and add garlic and green onion. Scrape up bits from bottom of pan. Add citrus sauce. Turn heat up to high and reduce sauce by half. Add chopped bok choy, salt and pepper to taste and sauté for 2–3 minutes. Add salmon fillets back to pan and heat with sauce for 1–2 minutes.

On plate, place noodles in center and top with piece of salmon. Ladle ½ cup of hot broth over fish and noodles. Spoon a few tablespoons of citrus sauce and bok choy over salmon. Garnish with chives (optional).

japanese citrus salmon with soba noodles and sautéed garlic bok choy

JAPANESE CITRUS SALMON WITH SOBA NOODLES AND SAUTÉED GARLIC BOK CHOY

This recipe calls for mango juice or mango puree. I suggest using products that are easily found at your local grocery store. Goya makes great mango juice and it's very inexpensive. If you want to use mango puree, thaw frozen mangos chunks and put 1 cup in blender with ⅓ cup water. Puree until smooth. The mango puree takes a few more steps, so if you're pressed for time, use mango juice.

Bok choy is an amazing vegetable. If you have never had bok choy, you will fall in love with it once you taste it. Bok choy has become popular in recent years and is used in many cooking applications because of its mild, crisp taste, and its versatility. It can be eaten raw in salads, or cooked in stir-fries, soups, and stews, or used as a side dish.

Another great quality of bok choy is its nutritional value. One half cup of raw Bok Choy contains only ten calories. Additionally, bok choy contains no fat or cholesterol and is a good source of calcium. It is also low in sodium and high in vitamins C and A. What's not to love, right? And the best thing is that it's very easy to prepare. Just wash the leafy stalks, chop, and eat raw or cook as desired.

What is zest? Zest is the outermost part of fruit peel. The white part is called the pith and is very bitter. So when "zesting," you want to only use the outermost layer of the fruit and not the white part. Why does a recipe call for zest? The zest is where you find all the essential aromatic oils of the fruit and they will bring an intense flavor to your recipes, hence the zest of the lemon in this recipe. Lemon and fish go so well together that the zest of the lemon will really bring your salmon to life and create an amazing, fresh, citrus flavor.

If you don't have a zester tool in your kitchen, you can use a cheese grater or peeler. Make sure you do not get the white part of the lemon when you are using these tools. Once you have grated or peeled the lemon, roughly chop the peel.

tuscan-style rigatoni with braised tomatoes, spinach, and italian sausage in light tomato-broth sauce

TUSCAN-STYLE RIGATONI WITH BRAISED TOMATOES, SPINACH, AND ITALIAN SAUSAGE IN LIGHT TOMATO-BROTH SAUCE

YIELD: 4 SERVINGS

1 lb. dry rigatoni pasta

2 tablespoons olive oil

1 teaspoon minced garlic

¼ cup green onion, chopped

½ cup yellow onion, diced small

¼ teaspoon red pepper flakes

⅔ cup cherry tomatoes, halved

¼ cup white wine

1 lb. bulk Italian sausage, cooked

⅔ cup chicken broth

2 tablespoons milk

1 heaping tablespoon tomato paste

¼ cup Parmesan cheese

pinch sugar

3 cups fresh spinach

salt and pepper to taste

Heat pot of water and cook pasta according to package instructions. For an al dente consistency, pull pasta a few minutes before package instructions states. Once cooked, drain pasta and toss with a little bit of olive oil to prevent noodles from sticking. Set aside.

Heat a large deep sauté pan on high with 2 tablespoons of olive oil. Add garlic, green onions, and yellow onions. Lower heat to medium-high and cook onions until soft and translucent. Add red pepper flakes and cherry tomatoes. Let tomatoes cook until tender. Add white wine, incorporate with other ingredients, and cook for another 3–4 minutes. Add Italian sausage, cooked pasta, and toss until combined. Cook for 4–5 minutes. Add chicken broth, milk, tomato paste, Parmesan, and sugar. Incorporate and cook for 4–5 minutes. Add spinach 1 cup at a time. Cook until it's wilted down, and repeat this process. Toss with other ingredients until all is combined and let cook for a few minutes. Salt and pepper to taste. Garnish with Parmesan cheese and drizzle with a little olive oil.

SCORE TIP:

TUSCAN-STYLE RIGATONI WITH BRAISED TOMATOES, SPINACH, AND ITALIAN SAUSAGE IN LIGHT TOMATO-BROTH SAUCE

This recipe is like all the dishes that I had in Italy. Simple ingredients are combined to pack a huge flavor punch. It's a very easy recipe to cook and takes less than 30 minutes to make. Hey, I kind of sound like Rachael Ray, don't I?

If you want to make this pasta al dente, pull pasta out of water a few minutes before the specified time on the package instructions. Al dente is an Italian expression that literally means "to the tooth." It refers to food that hasn't been overcooked and offers a little resistance (to the tooth) when you bite into it.

In this recipe, if you're watching your fat and calories, I would suggest using turkey or chicken sausage. You will get the same flavor but with less fat and calories. If my meat-and-potatoes-loving father, who doesn't like anything healthy, could not tell that I used turkey sausage in place of regular Italian sausage, your family and friends will not be able to either. Buonappetito!

Ex Number Six

Stewy and...

Fresh Herb-Encrusted Lamb Chops with Mint-Pea Puree and Rosemary-Tomato Couscous

No-Joke Smoked Chicken Chili

I can't tell you the whole story about this guy without creating a 300-page novel, so I'll give you the down and dirty details of this relationship. I met Stewy online. After all these online dating failures, you'd think I'd have realized this was not the way to meet men. Well, I didn't learn my lesson the first two or three times. On our first date, I met Stewy at a sushi place in Greenwich, Connecticut. He seemed very nice and energetic. We had a long dinner and the evening was a breath of fresh air. I thought I might actually have met the man of my dreams. The only thing I found a little odd was that he drank almost a bottle and a half of wine by himself. He was loaded when he left the sushi restaurant. As the night ended, we said our goodbyes, he gave me a very nice kiss, and I went on my merry way.

Over the next few weeks the relationship progressed quickly, but for some reason, I didn't mind. I loved the attention, gifts, and having someone to spend time with—who wouldn't? On our fourth date, Stewy decided to take me into New York City for dinner. He said he had the perfect Italian restaurant in mind and I would absolutely love it. So we drove into the city and parked the car around the corner from the restaurant. As we were walking toward it, I heard the sounds of a packed house. We walked into the place and there was not an inch of space. We squeezed into a few spots at the bar and had a good hour to kill before we got a table.

As we enjoyed a few glasses of wine, the music in the restaurant turned up to a decibel level that sounded as if we were in the front row at a rock concert. The song went from Frank Sinatra to Sir Mix-a-Lot's "Baby Got Back." Everyone in the restaurant jumped onto their chairs and started dancing as if they were at a college frat party.

I turned to Stewy with a look of fright and said, "Interesting place."

He laughed and said, "I knew you would love this place. Isn't it great?"

Yes, so great that the whole restaurant was filled entirely with drunk bachelorettes who sported condoms and lollipops on their "Suck-for-Bucks" shirts, celebrating the end of their freedom.

For the next three hours, this happened every thirty minutes. It was fun—the first time all the bachelorettes got on their chairs and shook their asses and attempted the white-man-with-an-overbite dance. (If you don't know this dance, Google or YouTube it.) Toward the end of the evening, "Ice Ice Baby" came on. Stewy, who was feeling nice and happy from the wine, jumped up on the chair and shimmied his shoulders like there was no tomorrow.

As crazy as it sounds, Stewy did help me create some stellar meals. One dish came to life one particularly cold evening: lamb chops encrusted in fresh herbs, mint pea puree, and rosemary-tomato couscous. I think Stewy's white-man-with-an-overbite dance inspired this.

FRESH HERB-ENCRUSTED LAMB CHOPS WITH MINT-PEA PUREE AND ROSEMARY-TOMATO COUSCOUS

YIELD: 4 SERVINGS

4 large lamb chops

¼ cup fresh parsley, chopped

¼ cup fresh mint, chopped

1 tablespoon fresh rosemary, chopped

1 tablespoon fresh basil, chopped

2 tablespoons stone ground mustard

¼ cup olive oil

1 teaspoon lemon juice

½ teaspoon salt

¼ teaspoon pepper

MINT PEA PUREE

1¼ cup chicken stock

¼ cup chopped carrots

¼ cup chopped onions

2½ cups frozen peas

⅛ teaspoon black pepper

½ teaspoon salt

¼ cup sour cream

1 tablespoon chopped fresh mint

1 teaspoon lemon juice

Preheat oven to 375 degrees.

In a small bowl, add all fresh herbs, mustard, olive oil, lemon juice, salt, and pepper. Blend together. Spread over each lamb chop. Set aside in fridge for 1 hour.

To make mint pea puree: In saucepan, place chicken stock, carrots, onions, frozen peas, pepper, and salt. Bring to boil and then reduce to simmer for 15 minutes.

Remove from heat and cool for 10 minutes. Add to food processor or blender, along with sour cream, mint, and lemon juice. Blend until smooth. Put back into saucepan and simmer on low, covered, for 10–15 minutes. Stir often.

Heat sauté pan with olive oil on high. Add lamb chops to very hot pan and sauté 3 minutes on each side until golden brown. Finish cooking in oven until medium consistency or desired doneness. Serve on top of mint pea puree. (To make this dish dairy free, eliminate sour cream.)

SCORE TIP:

FRESH HERB-ENCRUSTED LAMB CHOPS WITH MINT-PEA PUREE

Replace sour cream with silken, soft tofu if you're looking for a lower fat/calorie, dairy-free alternative. Replace with ⅓ cup soft tofu, which will still produce the same smooth, creamy feel in your mouth as sour cream.

ROSEMARY-TOMATO COUSCOUS

1 cup dried couscous

1- ¾ cup water

1 teaspoon apple cider vinegar

salt

1 tablespoon tomato paste

½ cup plain tomato sauce

1 teaspoon fresh rosemary, chopped fine

1 teaspoon balsamic

¼ teaspoon garlic salt

In medium saucepan, add couscous, water, salt, and apple cider vinegar. Bring to boil, stir, reduce heat to low simmer, and cover. Cook for 12–4 minutes until couscous is done and all water is absorbed. With heat still on medium-low, add rest of ingredients. Stir to combine and cook for another 7–8 minutes. Serve immediately.

For Valentine's Day, Stewy gave me the best present of them all—a Wii. At the time, Wii's were very hard to come by and it was the hottest item to have. I was ecstatic. This was the best present I had ever received. For the next several weeks, we played nonstop. On one particular night I was supposed to catch a flight to St. Louis for a business meeting, but it was canceled due to a massive blizzard. At the last minute I decided to have Stewy come up for dinner. I made no-joke smoked chicken chili, and trust me, this chili was no joke. Since the weather was so crappy, I used all the ingredients I had on hand to create this amazing chili. A chef always has an abundance of ingredients on hand.

After a fabulous meal we decided to break out the Wii. I was ready to kick some ass at tennis. We started playing and my tennis game started going down in flames fast. I became very frustrated that he was winning every single game, not to mention that he was rubbing in my face the fact that he was kicking my ass. I was pissed. I am a very competitive person and I hate to lose. We were on our nineteenth tennis match and when I served the ball with my Wii paddle, Stewy returned the ball. At this particular point I was standing very close to the TV and my marble fireplace. The ball came my way and I went full force with the swing, striking the side of the fireplace. Immediately I went down and an intense pain came rushing through my hand and fingers. Stewy looked at me in shock from the force of the hit, and then said, "Are you okay?" All I could do was cry because of the intense pain.

I looked at my fingers. The nail on my middle finger was completely black, severely swollen, and bloody. I had smashed my finger and it was bleeding very badly underneath the nail. To make a long story short, after a sleepless night in intense pain, I ended up in the ER the next morning. The ER doctor asked what had happened and when I explained how I had busted my finger, she said, "You would be surprised how many people come into the ER with Wii injuries." I was mortified. I was in the damn ER with a child's video game injury? After the resident-in-training drained the blood, gave me painkillers, and told me that I would be just fine, I wanted to go home and sleep.

As the week progressed and my pain subsided, I reduced my painkillers. But one day when I went to grab the pill bottle from my purse, I noticed the pills were all gone. All ten were missing. Who would have taken them? Did they fall into my purse? There was no sign of them anywhere and I was very suspicious.

Immediately I called Stewy. I asked if he had taken them, and he admitted that he had stolen them because he was addicted to pain medication. He told me he had been in and out of rehab for abusing pain medication and sleeping pills. *Oh my God*, I thought, *I'm dating—a druggie?!* I was mortified. I couldn't believe someone would steal from me, let alone lie. At this point, I decided to walk away from him and cut my losses. I guess things in life happen for a reason, and I had my guardian angels watching out for me.

no-joke smoked chicken chili

NO-JOKE SMOKED CHICKEN CHILI

YIELD: 4–6 SERVINGS

CHICKEN MARINADE

1 lb. chicken breasts, boneless, skinless, cubed

1 tablespoon smoked or sweet paprika

½ teaspoon ground black pepper

¼ teaspoon ground cayenne

1 teaspoon ground cumin

¼ cup dried parsley

¼ cup molasses

2 tablespoons honey

2 tablespoons balsamic vinegar

¼ cup olive oil

1 teaspoon liquid smoke (optional)

½ teaspoon salt

½ teaspoon garlic powder

1 teaspoon hot sauce

2 tablespoons olive oil

1 teaspoon garlic, chopped

⅓ cup green onions, chopped

1 small red onion, diced small

1 can black beans, drained

1 can kidney beans, drained

2 (15 oz.) cans diced tomatoes

4 vine-ripened tomatoes, quartered

1 teaspoon yellow mustard

salt and pepper to taste

cooked brown or white rice

In a large bowl, mix chicken marinade ingredients until all ingredients are incorporated and chicken is coated (first 14 ingredients). Set aside in fridge for 2 hours.

In medium stockpot, heat olive oil on high. Add garlic, green onions, and red onions. Lower heat to medium and sauté for 5–6 minutes. Add chicken mixture. Cook for 14–16 minutes and stir occasionally. In food processor or blender, add quartered tomatoes and pulse until slightly smooth. Add pureed tomatoes to the chicken mixture and the rest of the ingredients. Mix well until all ingredients are incorporated.

Bring to low simmer and cook for 45 minutes to 1 hour on low heat. Serve with brown rice.

Great for football parties!

SCORE TIP:

NO-JOKE SMOKED CHICKEN CHILI

I know you are looking at this recipe right now and saying, "That's a hell of lot of ingredients, Jenn." Yes, I will say it is a ton of ingredients, but your reward in the end will be great. I'm sure you have half the spices in you cabinet already and you haven't used them in years. See, I already saved you money and you can even do a little spice spring cleaning.

Smoked paprika is becoming a very popular spice in recipes today. If you have a hard time finding this spice, replace it with regular paprika or sweet paprika.

Ex Number Seven

Chaz and...

Roasted Red Pepper and Sun-Dried Tomato Bruschetta with Toasted Pine-Nut Puree, Topped with Goat Cheese Gremolata

Ginger, Tomato, Citrus Shredded Flank Steak with Pancetta Black Beans

As the dramatic chapter of my life in Connecticut was coming to an end, the drama with men reached its peak. If you thought all the other stories were funny and amusing, wait till you hear this one. I could have sworn this was an episode from *Sex and the City* and I was Carrie Bradshaw. This was my last go-round with online dating as my membership at a particular site was about to run out.

I met Chaz for our first date at a Starbucks. The date was good; we sat and talked for three hours. He gave me the typical first date rundown as to who he was. He worked for the government, was into weapon/gun training and martial arts, was a past bouncer at a few rap and strip clubs, hated sports, hadn't watched or owned a TV in five years, was into meditation, was the president of a Dungeon and Dragons role-playing group, and grew up in the beautiful state of Connecticut. What's not to love, right?

He called the next day to plan our second date. As we discussed ideas for our date, he mentioned that he was involved in a fire arms training class every month, and the day we were thinking of for our second date was when he had his class. He thought it would be a great idea to have our second date at the firearms training session. It was planned that I would shoot my first 9mm.

The day came and Chaz picked me up at my place. He was in his lovely attire of a *Star Wars* T-shirt, acid-washed jeans that were two sizes too small, and a pair of running shoes that looked as if they were twenty-two years old. As I went to hug him, I felt a gun and a large knife attached to his belt. Was he a government secret agent? I thought this was a little odd, but, what the hell, we were going to a firearms training class.

The class was filled with excops and military men. I watched for the first thirty minutes as they all went through their simulated drills. When it was my turn at the plate, the instructor took some time to familiarize me with a 9mm gun. I was scared as hell to shoot this thing, but with a little persuasion I was ready to blast away. What a rush when I fired the first shot! I felt like the most powerful person in the world at that moment. What a great stress reliever.

My high continued for weeks after the firearms class. Chaz mentioned that he wanted me to meet his parents. Wow! What a big step after dating for three weeks. It was Easter Sunday and Chaz's parents invited us to their lovely home in northern Connecticut for an Easter Sunday gourmet dinner.

We arrived around 4:00 p.m. Chaz's parents were in the driveway to greet us as we pulled in. His father was very friendly, kind, and welcoming. His mother looked at me as if I had three heads and seemed to wish me dead. I just brushed off her reaction because that was the behavior of the majority of people in Connecticut.

As we settled down in their lovely country home and dinner was almost ready, I asked if she needed help with anything, and she gave me a very quick, stern no. It was interesting that Chaz didn't comment on his mother's behavior; he seemed to think it was normal. We sat down to dinner and the menu was as dull and tasteless as the mother: salty ham that tasted as if it were from a can; lumpy, pasty, mashed potatoes; peas that were seasoned with steam; corn from a can; salad from a bag and enough soy milk to feed the state of Texas. Worst of all, his parents didn't drink, so there was neither wine nor cocktails to drown the uncomfortable feelings I had.

After asking me general background questions as I sat on the witness stand, the mother, who already loved me to death, asked me what my religion was. I told her politely that I was a Catholic and thought how unbelievably rude she was to ask this question of someone she didn't know. Chaz just sat back in his chair and didn't say a word to his mother, who proceeded to ask me what type of house my parents lived in. What kind of question is that? Once again I answered politely, "A two-story house in Cleveland." Again, Chaz sat lifeless and the father just smiled. I asked the mother about her background and where she grew up. She said she grew up in Arkansas and moved to Connecticut when she was in her twenties. Chaz chimed in, "Yeah, she used to carry a loaded gun in her purse everywhere she went. You never know in those backwoods of Arkansas what's going to happen." The whole family laughed, and a nervous laugh came from my mouth.

After the lightning round of questions, I helped clean and clear the table. The mother told Chaz and me to go sit and relax. I took my cup of tea to the living room, and Chaz and his father took the dogs outside. There I was, alone with the she-devil. She disappeared upstairs for a few minutes and when she returned, she sat right next to me with a whole shoe box full of photos. She started showing me photos of her beloved Chaz when he was younger. I really didn't know what to think about this whole thing, but I played along and acted as if I enjoyed the nostalgia. She showed me a few pictures of Chaz that were rather embarrassing for him. He was about seven or eight years old and he was in a bright turquoise, sequined, satin, sailor unitard with shiny, black, patent-leather tap shoes and glitter leg warmers. His little faced looked so mortified in the photo.

At 8:00 p.m. it was time to go. I told Chaz I had a long, early-morning run and I needed to get going. He told his parents I had a ten-mile run in the morning and we had to leave. The mother looked at me with the ugliest scowl and said, "Why would you do that? Run. That's dumb."

Wow! I felt the love at that very moment.

As the drama evolved, I created some fantastic recipes during my relationship with Chaz. Ginger, tomato, citrus, shredded flank steak with pancetta black beans and roasted red pepper and sun-dried tomato bruschetta with a toasted pine-nut puree, topped with goat cheese gremolata.

We didn't last for two weeks after the family "sit down." The relationship fizzled and I reached my breaking point. I'd had enough of men in the North East and most importantly, the state of Connecticut. After my dramatic, unfulfilled, painful, and immature relationships, I was off to the fabulous windy city to live. Arrivederci, Connecticut. You will not be missed.

roasted red pepper and sun-dried tomato bruschetta with toasted pine-nut puree, topped with goat cheese gremolata

ROASTED RED PEPPER AND SUN-DRIED TOMATO BRUSCHETTA WITH TOASTED PINE-NUT PUREE, TOPPED WITH GOAT CHEESE GREMOLATA

1 baguette

olive oil

salt

1 cup roasted red peppers, drained

½ cup sun-dried tomatoes, packed in olive oil

1 medium-sized garlic glove, smashed

2 teaspoons balsamic vinegar

1 tablespoon olive oil

⅓ cup fresh basil leaves

salt and pepper

1 cup pine nuts

salt and pepper

2–3 tablespoons olive oil

⅓ cup goat cheese crumbles

½ cup fresh parsley, chopped

¼ cup lemon zest

2 teaspoons fresh garlic, chopped fine

Preheat oven to 375 degrees.

Slice baguette into ¼-inch-thick slices. Put on baking sheet, brush with olive oil, and season with salt and pepper. Bake until light golden brown for 20–25 minutes. Cool and set aside.

In food processor or blender, add roasted red peppers, sun-dried tomatoes, garlic, vinegar, basil, olive oil, salt, and pepper. Blend until smooth. Put in container and set aside in fridge.

In medium sauté pan on medium-high heat, place pine nuts, salt, and pepper. Shake pan consistently to agitate pine nuts so they don't burn. When nuts are lightly browned, remove from heat and cool on plate. When nuts have cooled, place in food processor or blender with olive oil. Blend until smooth. Add more oil if pine nut mixture is too thick. Add salt to taste. Put in bowl and set aside.

In small bowl, crumble goat cheese. Add parsley, garlic, and lemon zest. Blend together. Set aside.

Place 2 teaspoons pine-nut spread on baguette slices. Top with 1 tablespoon bruschetta mixture and top that with 1 teaspoon goat cheese mixture. Repeat. Serve immediately.

ROASTED RED PEPPER AND SUN-DRIED TOMATO BRUSCHETTA WITH TOASTED PINE-NUT PUREE, TOPPED WITH GOAT CHEESE GREMOLATA

A gremo— what? Gremolata is an Italian condiment that consists of chopped parsley, garlic, and lemon zest. It is usually served with osso bucco Milanese, an Italian veal dish. Gremolata can be used in other recipes as well and is very versatile. It can bring a refreshing flavor to really heavy meat dishes and can pack a great punch with seafood dishes. When using raw garlic, a little bit goes a long way. I like to add a little olive oil to smooth out the pungent taste of the garlic. In this recipe, I add goat cheese and this really balances all the flavors and makes for a tasty garnish.

Note: This recipe is to die for, but the rule of thumb is that if you're cooking for a first date, cut back on the garlic tremendously.

GINGER, TOMATO, CITRUS SHREDDED FLANK STEAK WITH PANCETTA BLACK BEANS

YIELD: 4–6 SERVINGS

2–2½ lb. flank steak

2 tablespoons olive oil

2 tablespoons chopped fresh ginger

1 teaspoon garlic, chopped

⅓ cup green onions, chopped

1 cup beef broth

1 (28 oz.) can stewed, chopped tomatoes

⅓ cup cilantro leaves and stems

1 tablespoon fresh chives, chopped

½ cup ketchup

1 teaspoon hot sauce

½ cup orange juice

1 lemon, juiced

1 tablespoon apple cider vinegar

PANCETTA BEANS

1 tablespoon olive oil

½ cup pancetta, chopped

1 green pepper, top, bottom, and seeds removed, chopped

¼ cup yellow onion, chopped

2 (15 oz.) cans black beans, drained

⅓ cup beef broth

1 lime, squeezed

Preheat oven to 325 degrees.

In medium stockpot, heat olive oil on high. Add garlic, ginger, and green onions and lower heat to medium-high. Sauté for 2–3 minutes and do not burn garlic. Add flank steak and brown on both sides for 3–4 minutes per side.

Add the rest of the braise ingredients and mix all together. Bring mixture to boil. Cover with lid and put pot in oven for 2–3 hours until meat shreds easily with fork. Season with salt and pepper to taste.

Take flank steak out of braising mixture and set on cutting board. Allow to rest for 2 minutes. Bring braising liquid to full, rolling boil. Reduce liquid to 1 cup. Shred flank steak with forks. When liquid has been reduced, add shredded flank steak back to pot and incorporate in liquid. Heat throughout and serve with pancetta beans.

To make pancetta beans: In medium saucepan, heat olive oil on high. Add pancetta, reduce heat to medium-high, and cook until crisp. Add green peppers and onions, and cook for 6-minutes, until soft. Add beans and broth. Mix together and cook for 12–15 minutes. Squeeze lime into bean mixture, mix, and turn off heat. Serve immediately with ginger, tomato, citrus shredded flank steak. Garnish with fresh cilantro leaves.

SCORE TIP:

GINGER, TOMATO, CITRUS SHREDDED FLANK STEAK WITH PANCETTA BLACK BEANS

I enjoyed a dish similar to this recipe when I lived in Connecticut. I went on numerous first dates to this particular Cuban place where I always ordered this dish. Needless to say, the restaurant is still going strong whereas those first dates fizzled before the first course. The memory of this particular dish really stands out in my mind because of the amazing fresh flavors that are combined together. I never thought that ginger and tomato would work so well together.

When I came up with my own version of this dish, I added some citrus flavors to really bring out the flavor of the ginger and tomato.

I slowly braise the flank steak for 2-3 hours so it absorbs every flavor. Low and slow is the name of the game in this recipe—low oven temp and a slow cooking time, that is. (Get your mind out of the gutter, Jenn.)

Ex Number Eight

Stephan and...

Thai Coconut Chicken Soup

Stoker Shrimp Cakes with Hearts of Palm-Avocado Salad and Creole Mustard Vinaigrette

It was right after the second biggest challenge of my life: running my second marathon. I successfully completed the race forty-five minutes faster than my prior marathon. You bet I wore that medal proudly. For three days, I wore that medal everywhere. Everyone thought I was a lost, lonely Olympic athlete, still confused about when the Beijing Olympics ended. I sparked a romance with a great guy right after the marathon; we clicked immediately. Jason was in the hospitality field and we understood each

other's worlds all too well. Before I started dating Jason, my girlfriend, Annette, mentioned that she had a great European guy she wanted to set me up with, but I was focused on the marathon and my new romance with Jason and totally forgot about the Euro "fix-up." In early November, I got a phone call from a gentleman who spoke with a very thick, foreign accent. When he introduced himself, I knew right away he was Annette's Euro "fix up" friend. At this point, I was very involved with Jason and didn't want to go out with the European, but when he asked me out for dinner, I tentatively agreed after seeing a photo of him. Two days before the date, I contemplated canceling. On the day of the date, I texted the European to ask how long the date would take. Wow! If that doesn't scream excitement about the date, I don't know what does.

The first few dates with Stephan were great, but I still had a lingering guilt about seeing someone behind Jason's back. That wasn't who I was or the kind of thing I did. But the more time I spent with Stephan, the more I enjoyed his company. We shared a lot in common; running was the biggest part of our lives. After we spent another night out, Stephan asked me to run with him and his running group on Saturday morning. I was rather excited to join a running group. I wanted to meet more people in Chicago since I had just moved there.

Bright and early on Saturday morning, I met Stephan and his group at their usual meeting spot, a massive metal statue of an old man sitting on a chair, a block away from the lake. I was introduced to Stew, who was Stephan's partner in crime, aka godfather. He had the sharpest, most sarcastic tongue in Chicago, creator of the Saturday Run/Brunch Club and the best chorizo-chili maker in Chicago. Mullad, aka Madman was Saudi Arabian born and loved to run ultra-adventure marathons around the world for the hell of it without doing any formal training. His favorite running temperature was over 90 degrees, and he was always sporting the just-rolled-out-of-bed head. Frank, the "Caucasian Kenyan," ran alone because none of the others could keep up with his lightning-fast pace. He could run anyone under the table and only ran short distances with no desire to do a marathon. Chuck was a tall, lanky, quirky, soft-spoken Canadian who drank like an Irishman and could stumble out of bed, still drunk from the night before, and yet maintain his running poise. Olivia was the bombshell with the face of a cover model, a Boston Marathon qualifier, and a running

machine. Carolina, the Chilean femme fatale, was tough as nails. She ran the last half of the Santiago Marathon in 90-degree temperatures with a severely injured Achilles tendon and crossed the finish line. Johnnie, aka Marbles, was the Italian stallion, fast-talking, South-Side Chicagoan who had a passion for running and was a perpetual "maybe" whenever he was invited to any events. Finally, Tallulah, the Scottish-born endurance machine who could drink anyone under the table, was the American version of Bridget Jones. She partied like a rock star and could still get up the next morning and run twenty miles without any complaints. These were the crazy characters who would eventually become my dearest, closest friends.

As I learned on my first day with the group, it was all about the brunch after the run. This was a big part of the Saturday morning ritual and food seemed to be the center of it all. Agenda: Run for an hour or so, then eat for two hours. What's not to like, right? Sign me up! As I mentioned in the beginning of the book, it's all about the food and how it brings people together to create memories for life.

There comes a time in a gal's life when she has to choose the right thing do. That thing, for me, was to decide which relationship I was going to break off. As I grew closer to Stephan, I decided to break up with Jason. It wasn't easy and I felt like the world's worst person, but I couldn't hide my intense feelings for the European. "Here goes nothing," I said to myself. And off I went into the arms of Stephan.

As Christmas approached, I established a great relationship with the European and I was having the time of my life. I grew closer to the group of runners and made some great friendships. On one particular Saturday morning, over our usual brunch, Stew asked if we would be interested in running in the Santa Speedo run. Now, I was trying to wrap my brain around what Stew was saying: Speedo, outside, cold, race, and no clothes. Was this an actual race in the dead of winter in the windy city? Well, apparently my crazy ass signed up for it along with Stew, Stephan, Johnnie, and Chuck.

On the day of the skin-to-win race, we had our normal run in the morning, along with a hearty, warm brunch, and after that we were off to the bar where the race began. Yes, the starting line was at a bar. Come on, you had to do something to numb the pain as you ran 1.2 miles down Michigan Avenue in your skivvies on a very cold, windy, Chicago day. I was smart about how I was going to run and still maintain some sort of warmth. I wore a running skirt, black sports bra, and my arm warmers. I know it wasn't very Christmassy, but I would be ahead of the game. My partners in crime wore full-blown, bright red Speedos. Both Stephan and Stew represented the United States of America well: red and blue Speedos and white skin—very patriotic. As we all indulged in noon-time cocktails, we geared up for the short, fast run. It was a balmy 82 degrees inside the bar. The outside temperature was 18 degrees. The MC rallied the 150 participants and instructed us to strip down to our next-to-nothing attire. The unofficial race would start inside the bar. All of us crazy runners would file onto the Chicago streets, and we would endure a 1.2 mile run down Michigan Avenue among the holiday tourists. When the cold air hit my exposed white skin, I actually didn't feel any pain. I think it was Mr. Bud Light and the shots of whiskey that helped out. I felt great. When we all had to stop and wait to cross a busy intersection, some of the other participants in their shiny Speedos starting doing pushups and squat thrusts to stay warm. The stunned, perplexed looks on the innocent bystanders' faces were priceless. I'm sure if you go on YouTube you will see many videos from that day. Ah, what a day to remember.

It was Christmas Eve, and my plan was to cook for Stew and Stephan. The dynamic trio would be together on a very special night. My dinner for the boys would not be a traditional Christmas Eve dinner.

I made Thai chicken coconut soup and a few types of sushi with fresh Chicago Ahi tuna and salmon. I showed my two sous chefs how to roll sushi, and I was very impressed by their rolling skills. For some reason, we thought we were preparing a meal for ten people because we had so much food. After we settled our full bellies with a funny Christmas movie, Stew wanted to watch another movie. It was well into the wee hours of Christmas morning and the sexual tension between Stephan and me was at an all-time high. Stew popped in the next DVD and not five minutes into the movie, Stephan and I both stood up and said it was time to leave. Maybe the sushi we had made and eaten had the same effect as raw oysters. I can confirm that to be true. The drive back was the fastest drive I had ever experienced from the South Side of Chicago to Lakeview. We were there in less than ten minutes. We practically had all our clothes off by the time we made it into Stephan's apartment.

Being as cute as he was, I had overlooked the fact that he lived in a 1940s, never-updated, hole in the wall. It was rather creepy because there were bugs crawling around in the dead of winter.

As the holiday season festivities continued, Stephan's best friends came to Chicago all the way from Hungary. Zsolt and Tamis were two characters I will never forget. For two people who had not been to the United States before, their English was very good and they were the sweetest yet wildest bunch of guys I had ever met. Oh, and did I mention, they both were ridiculously good looking? What a great week ahead of me, spending time with three sexy, hot, European men. Lucky me.

During Stephan's friends' visit to the Windy City, I helped him play tour guide. We must have gone to every tourist spot imaginable in the Chicago area: museums, Navy pier, Willis (Sears) Tower, John Hancock building, Michigan Avenue, Al Capone's old hangout, and every Starbucks café. We even got the boys out on the frigid lake path one snowy morning for a short six-mile run. Needless to say, they stopped off at the nearest coffee shop around mile two to indulge in some espressos while the rest of us finished our run.

Their second-to-last night in the States was New Year's Eve and we were set to cook dinner before we went to drink the night away. I was going to teach the chef of the group, Zsolt, how to make a few dishes so he could take the recipes back to Hungary and teach his fellow Hungarians some killer American dishes.

While the boys were here, they kept talking about the guacamole that they had eaten at one of the Mexican joints in the Old Towne area. They had never had such a thing, and I decided to show Zsolt how to make it so he could take the recipe back to Hungary. He was impressed that such simple ingredients in the guacamole could taste that good when all mixed together. I also taught Zsolt how to make a basic chili recipe—something like my smoked chicken chili recipe—and my famous shrimp cakes. As we were cooking together, he talked about various Hungarian dishes and how different they were from recipes here in the USA. He talked about how his mom and grandmother cooked every meal from scratch and how simple the recipes were. Some Hungarian dishes that were his favorites; Goulash, Chicken Paprikash, Jókai bean soup, and Somloi galuska.

After the holidays, a small group of us runners decided to go skiing in Northern Wisconsin. I know. I didn't even know Wisconsin had hills, let alone a ski resort. Our chariot rolled up to my place at 4:00 a.m. Stew had rented a massive SUV the size of my entire apartment. It was pimped out and we were ready to roll up to Wisconsin. Dean and Johnnie were already inside the car fast asleep when Stephan and I climbed in. As we drove out of my apartment driveway, Stew cranked up the stereo and the uncensored version of Lil Jon's "Skeet Skeet" filled the car.

After the five-hour drive up north to Wisconsin, we arrived at the ski resort. We all suited up in our ski gear and were ready to hit the slope. As you can see, I said, "slope," because that's what it was: one very large hill. Stephan, Stew, and I headed up on the lift to conquer the big hill while Dean and Johnnie tried out snowboarding for the first time. Needless to say, as we were going up on the lift, the Shawn White wanna-bes were in front of us. They attempted to get off the lift and ended up tangled underneath. They stopped the lift. After our thirty-ninth run down the massive hill, we all were ready to call it a day, especially Dean and Johnnie with their battered and bruised bodies.

The first forty-five minutes of the car ride back were silent. Stew was cranky because he was driving back in dense fog and doing his sixth hour of driving on his birthday. Stephan was hungry and growing cranky. Dean was lost in his own little world, and Johnnie was in the front seat fully awake and playing DJ with the radio. From the far back of the massive SUV, I faintly heard a deep voice say something. I thought it was the radio, so I paid no attention. I heard this same sound again.

"What the hell was that?"

Stephan was texting Stew from the back seat, asking him how much further we had to go. Stew yelled back at Stephan, "Really dude, you're texting me from the back seat?"

As we got closer and closer to Chicago, the sound of the deep voice became more frequent until Stew yelled at Johnnie, "What the hell is that sound?"

Johnnie replied, "That's my cell phone, man. It's Mr. T saying, 'Shut up, fool.'"

Johnnie's phone had been going off every two minutes with Mr. T's voice saying, "Shut up, fool." Finally, Stew lost it and threatened Johnnie. He was going to throw him and his phone out the window if he didn't turn off the Mr. T voice. Needless to say, the Chicago skyline couldn't come soon enough.

My short relationship with Mr. Euro ended when he confessed that he only wanted a convenient, sexual relationship with me. It was a major slap in the face and broke my heart into a-million-and-one pieces. I can say that I am thankful for meeting him, though. I would have never met all of the great friends I have now if it had not been for Stephan. And ladies, if you ever visit or live in the Chicago area, be very wary of the good-looking European man with a thick accent. He may be great to look at and hook you in with his charismatic, charming ways, but his immature, spoiled-rotten personality will force you to put him in time-out and enroll him in the nearest mommy-and-me daycare.

thai coconut chicken soup

THAI COCONUT CHICKEN SOUP
YIELD: 4 SERVINGS

SOUP

1 (15 oz.) can coconut milk

1 (15 oz.) can lite coconut milk

1 ½ tablespoon Thai roasted chili paste (Allergen alert: contains shrimp paste)

1–2 teaspoons hot chili oil (depending on your level of heat)

1 lime, juiced

3–4 small to medium chicken breasts

½ cup chopped cilantro

1 ½ cup chicken stock

GARNISH

½ cup chopped roasted peanuts

⅓ cup chopped cilantro

2 cups snow peas

2 cups fresh bean sprouts

1½ cups chopped carrots

cooked rice noodles

In medium saucepan, incorporate all soup ingredients except for raw chicken and bring to boil. Add chicken and reduce heat to medium boil. Depending on how hot you want your soup, you can always add more hot chili oil.

Cook covered for 45 minutes to 1 hour, or until chicken falls apart with a fork. Take pan off heat and remove chicken to a plate with tongs or fork. With two forks, shred chicken. Add chicken back into coconut liquid. Put back onto burner and bring to simmer. In bowls, add cooked rice noodles, snow peas, bean sprouts, and carrots. Ladle soup mixture over noodles and vegetables. Top with chopped peanuts and garnish with cilantro.

THAI COCONUT CHICKEN SOUP

I can confirm that every time I make this simple recipe for anyone, I receive nothing but rave reviews. Three ingredients that really make this recipe are roasted chili paste, coconut milk, and hot chili oil. The roasted chili paste and hot chili oil can usually be found in the Asian aisle at your local grocery store. The key is to use regular (classic) coconut milk and light coconut milk. I made the mistake of using just light coconut milk when I made this for my mom and the taste was not that great. I know that coconut milk has a lot of fat, but it's well worth it. This is a great dish to impress and knock the socks off anyone.

STOKER SHRIMP CAKES WITH HEARTS OF PALM-AVOCADO SALAD AND CREOLE MUSTARD VINAIGRETTE

1 lb. raw shrimp, peeled and deveined

¼ cup green onions, chopped

1 tablespoon fresh chives, chopped

1 teaspoon mustard

1½–2 cups saltine crackers, crushed very fine

1 teaspoon hot sauce

1 lemon, squeezed

⅓ cup mayo

1 egg, well beaten

1 cup panko bread crumbs

⅓ cup flour

¼ cup olive oil

In food processor, pulse shrimp until it becomes a chunky paste (10 pulses). In large bowl, add shrimp, green onions, chives, crackers, mayo, mustard, hot sauce, and lemon juice. Mix and fold together until all ingredients are blended. If mixture is too wet, add more crushed crackers.

In standard breading fashion, place well-beaten egg into one bowl, flour in a second bowl, and panko in a third bowl. Form shrimp mixture into small patties, ¼ inch thick. Dip into flour and shake off excess. Next, dip into egg wash and finally, coat with panko bread crumbs. Place on plate. Repeat this process until all shrimp mixture is gone. Put in freezer for 30 minutes. In sauté pan, heat olive oil until pan is smoking. Sauté cakes until golden brown on each side, 6–8 minutes per side. Turn heat to medium-high. Serve with hearts of palm salad.

HEARTS OF PALM-AVOCADO SALAD

1 can/jar hearts of palm, drained and cut into small, bite-sized pieces

½ cup fresh mango, diced small

1 small red pepper, diced small

1 tablespoon fresh cilantro, chopped

1 avocado, peeled, pit removed,

diced small

¼ cup green onion, chopped

salt and pepper

In large bowl, combine all ingredients. Add Creole mustard dressing and combine.

CREOLE MUSTARD VINAIGRETTE

¼ cup cider vinegar

1 tablespoon Creole mustard

1 tablespoon orange juice

¼ teaspoon sugar

½ teaspoon garlic, chopped

½ teaspoon hot sauce

¼ cup olive oil

salt and pepper to taste

¼ teaspoon dried thyme, chopped

1 tablespoon cilantro, chopped

Combine the vinegar, mustard, orange juice, sugar, hot sauce, and garlic. Mix well. Whisk in the olive oil. Season with salt, pepper, and hot sauce. Add the herbs. Season with salt and pepper to taste. Chill for a few hours before serving.

SCORE TIP:

CREOLE MUSTARD VINAIGRETTE

Creole mustard is a variation of whole-grain mustard in which the seeds are slightly crushed. If you can't find Creole mustard in your local grocery store, you can substitute any type of coarse, grainy mustard.

There are two basic styles of mustard: those that are smooth and those that contain whole or roughly ground seeds of the mustard plant. I prefer the more textured mustards. I think the flavor is more intense and adds more depth to your recipes. So leave the yellow mustard for your hot dogs.

Ex Number Nine

L&D and...

Tater Tot Nachos

Cotton Candy Martini

My wild and crazy journey continues down the road through the endless town of Singlesville. I swore off online dating and said I would never, ever go back because there were too many bizarre characters. I hadn't met anyone of quality; it was more like quantity, which I wasn't looking for. As corny and cheesy as it sounds, I really wanted to find my true love in life. Despite all these stories of my exes that have accrued over time, I still haven't lost hope. At least, not yet.

My arm was twisted to the highest degree by my

girlfriends because I wasn't going on any dates and most of my Friday and Saturday nights consisted of working on this book. I broke down and my online dating account was reinstated. Right off the bat I hit it off with a fella we will call L&D (aka Lovely and Delicious). I will explain how his nick name came about later in the story. L&D was the mildly attractive, older, ego-driven co-owner of an investment trading firm, who lived in an affluent North Shore neighborhood, was divorced, had three kids, two in college and one in high school, and his favorite thing to do was talk about himself.

On our first date we met at a wine, cheese, and chocolate bar on Michigan Avenue. I worked all day at my office on Michigan Avenue. I walked more than eight blocks in temperatures below 20 degrees to the lobby of a beautiful hotel attached to the wine bar. L&D came across town from the Willis Tower (formerly Sears Tower), where, as he had already told me ten times, he had an office.

As I tried to defrost my body and blow my red nose into a crumpled old tissue, in walks L&D with his arms out.

"Hello Jenn, very nice to finally meet you."

We hugged and he said, "Have you ever been in this building?"

"No, I haven't."

He was taken aback that I had never been in that historical building, let alone never taken a tour of the place.

"Well you're in luck. I've been in this building plenty of times. Let me show you around."

After Tom-the-Tour-Director had shown me around the historical building and given me a brief Chicago history lesson, we headed to the wine bar. I was ready for a glass of vino, stat! We each ordered a flight of wine and some spicy olives to munch on. I told him that I only had a few hours before I had to leave and go pick up my child, Carlton, at Doggie Daycare. No judging. I'm sure there are a lot of you out there who take your dogs to daycare. We went through the standard first date questions and learned what we could about one another within a few hours.

At the end of our date, outside on the busy street, he leaned in, kissed, and hugged me goodbye, and said, "You are absolutely lovely, and so delicious. I would love to see you again."

Delicious? What did that mean? I thought about how odd that comment was but accepted his invitation to see him again. He asked how far my walk back to my office was and I told him it was about eight blocks. He flagged down a cab, and I thought, "Oh how nice, he's going to drop me off first, then head to Union Station to catch his train back to fairy-tale land. But no, that wasn't the case.

He said, "Sorry, I'm in a hurry to catch the train. Had a great time. Gotta run, babe. Call you tomorrow."

I stood there stunned, turned into the cold, blustery Chicago wind, and watched L&D drive off in a warm cab. I walked eight blocks back to my car in three-inch heels.

After our initial wine date, his text messages were too much. I'm sure it is every girl's dream to get texts like this after the first date, but when you really aren't "into someone," they can be downright creepy. Because we'd only known each other for a few hours, his messages didn't add up. Some examples are: "I could spend the rest of my life with you. You are so delicious and lovely." "Hey, guess what. I'm thinking about you." I guessed he was either a hopeless romantic or just wanted to score with me as soon as possible.

The weekend was near and my girlfriend, Norma Jean, (yes, her parents were a little obsessed with Marilyn Monroe) and I were throwing an 80s theme party. We were going to make all the different foods from our childhood and turn them into gourmet dishes. From SpaghettiOs dip, Steak-Umm sliders, Tater Tot nachos, cotton candy martinis with a Pop Rocks rim, MicroMagic fries with a curry-chipotle dip, chocolate dipped Twinkies, ring pops, and the list goes on and on.

I told Norma about L&D and asked her, "Do you think I should invite him? Would that be a ballsy move?"

She said, "What the hell! Invite this lovely and

delicious guy."

Well, I was not really thinking straight at the time—because this would be our second date. Wow! What a second date this is going to be, right? The day before the party I called L&D and asked if he'd like to come to the party.

He said, "Yes, I would definitely like to come and be your date. What should I bring?"

I told him to bring a bottle of vino and we'd have the rest covered.

The day of party came and by the time the party had started, Norma and I were already loaded up on Pixie Sticks, cotton candy martinis, and Pop Rocks. Our nerves were revved up like a bunch of kindergarteners on a sugar high.

As our guests arrived and settled in with cotton candy martinis, the buzzer sounded. L&D had arrived. I buzzed him in and he was greeted by Carlton. I always like to test out how the guy is around dogs and Carlton is the perfect bait for that. He was very warm to Carlton's greeting. He gave me a Hollywood-type kiss right when he walked in the door as if we'd been dating for the past year. I introduced L&D to all my friends, and he had that typical politician air about him. Confident, arrogant, observant, full of answers, and self-absorbed. I'm sure if there had been a few babies at the party, he would have tossed them up and down like sacks of flour.

During the party, L&D felt right at home, so at home he was attached to my side, affectionately kissing and massaging my neck and draping himself all over me like a mammoth python getting ready to strangle its victim. I felt as if I was at a college frat party and we were making out in front of everyone. I really didn't have any concerns at this point about my friends witnessing this behavior because I was full to the brim with cotton candy martinis and skinny-girl margaritas. I was feeling no pain.

The night progressed and there was this odd "bad" energy in the air. I had this miniature stuffed chicken on top of my stove and somehow it fell into the cheese sauce that topped the Tator Tot nachos. I noticed the chicken in the cheese and all hell started breaking loose. My girlfriend, Sara, was trying to set up her Xbox behind the TV and tripped into my fireplace mantel. I'm not sure if she'd had one too many martinis or if it was the curse of the chicken. Norma Jean was juggling a few men in her life and sent the wrong text message to the wrong fella, and well, that didn't end well with guy number one. Curse of the chicken falling in the cheese? I was in the back bedroom and L&D was telling me how he could see himself falling in love with me. My replied, "Ah, I am having fun with you and you are too kind." As I spoke those words to him, I patted him on the back as if he were a little kid who had just earned his first A+ on a homework assignment.

The party started to wind down and little by little, our friends started to leave. It was already 2:00 a.m., and Norma Jean was horizontal on the couch. I told her she couldn't leave because I knew L&D wanted to spend the night and as far as I was concerned he wasn't about to take that next step into Pootangland. My intentions were to get him out of my place, but he wasn't leaving. When he finally got the hint, he strolled over to Norma Jean with a Rico Sauvé swag, kissed her on the cheek, and said, "Thanks again for all the food, it was so delicious. You are so lovely." Norma Jean said her goodbyes with an odd look on her face and when he walked toward the door, she gave me a face as if she smelled something really bad.

The third date came and went and more over-the-top texts about "being his wife," "being the one," and his famous saying, "Hey, guess what. I'm thinking about you, baby." I think it was the way he said this line because when you're really into someone, it's always nice to know that person is thinking about you, but from L&D it was rather creepy.

For our fourth date, we decided to make dinner

together. The forty-five-minute drive up the North Shore was rather scenic. Being a city dweller, I welcomed the peacefulness of the area. It was as if I'd stepped into another dimension and had landed in a foreign country. Compared to the insane, chaotic, noisy, high-energy city, this was a vacation.

I pulled up to his house. It was a nice, newer home with a three-car garage and no neighbors in sight. As I got out of the car to collect all my groceries from the trunk, the side door opened and a teenaged kid appeared.

"Oh, good Lord, please don't say that's his son," I mumbled.

Lo and behold, it was his son on his way to a high-school track practice. He greeted me with a cold smile and said hello. I introduced myself and he asked if I needed help carrying my groceries in.

I introduced him to Carlton and he said, "Oh, how lovely. I'm not a dog person."

Not sure what to comment at that point, I politely said okay.

As the son left, L&D pulled into the drive way in his ten-year-old Range Rover smiling from ear to ear. He got out of his car and said, "So you met my son, Tyler."

I decided to make Thai and when I rattled off the menu to L&D, he appeared to be lost after the words lemon grass, sriacha, and fish sauce. He asked me, "So, do you have enough for three?"

Three of us? I guess I just got recruited to cook for the family. I didn't mind, but I really just wanted a dinner for the two of us so I could get to know Mr. L&D a little more.

As I marinated the salmon in lemon grass, soy sauce, fresh ginger, and a little bit of fish sauce, I put L&D

to work on the vegetables for the Vietnamese spring rolls. The rice was cooking on the stove in coconut milk, ginger, lemon grass, and a hint of sugar in the raw. The sesame-oil-coated bok choy and fennel were grilling nicely on the stove when all of sudden L&D starting doing these bizarre stretching poses in the middle of kitchen. He said that he'd had such a tough workout week that he was cramping up. Two spin classes and few short runs on the treadmill qualify as "tough" workouts I guessed. It sounded as if he were at the height of his training for the Kona Ironman.

I smiled politely and said, "I'm sure you will be okay."

He grabbed me and said, "Hey, guess what."

I could fill in the blank and answer his question, but I played along and said, "What?"

"I really dig you, and I'm thinking about you."

As we proceeded to make out in the kitchen, he pushed me into the fridge and kissed me with a very heavy, sloppy mouth and tongue. We heard the garage door opening and his son coming back home. Immediately we composed ourselves and the son walked in and said, "What's for dinner?"

I told him I was making Thai and dinner would be ready in five minutes. A chef always wants to please her audience with her food no matter who they are. The son and L&D were very happy and plates were cleaned.

Score.

L&D and I cleaned up the kitchen and the son went immediately upstairs. We decided to watch a movie, well, not really. It was just on in the background while we made out on the couch. Even for an older guy, he was raring to go. I decided to stay the night because I'd had one too many glasses of wine. He led me upstairs to his "palace" as he called it. The "palace" was grand. Everything was larger than life, just like his ego. His bed was so massive I had to literally make a running leap into the thing.

In the morning, I had luggage underneath my eyes because I was so tired from not sleeping. I was up all night because L&D had snored like a dirty truck driver who had been out all night drinking at the strip clubs. It was Friday and I had taken a personal day off. L&D was getting ready to head into the city by train.

I was in a daze when L&D got up and said in a very perky voice, "Good morning, beautiful. Would you like some coffee?"

As I proceeded to say yes please, he told me the long story about how wonderful his coffee was and how rare the brand was. I looked at him as if he were speaking another language. Not really caring where the coffee came from, I just wanted something hot, brown, and loaded with caffeine.

He left to head downstairs and I realized the son was still sleeping. I did not want his son to see me leave the house. I needed to leave very quickly and quietly. I knew the walk of shame was right around the corner. I had to get out of there.

We fooled around a bit as the coffee perked me up and L&D jumped out of bed and into the shower. As I started getting dressed, I heard L&D singing the Beach Boys song "Good Vibrations" as if he were auditioning for a spot on the senior edition of *American Idol*.

I tiptoed downstairs to collect my belongings and get Carlton ready to go. I did not want to wake the sleeping giant.

On a scale from 1 to 10, I was scoring a big fat 1 for the sexiest woman alive award. My hair looked like

a bomb had hit it. My makeup was smeared, and I desperately needed to brush my teeth. The walk of shame was near. Hey, no judging! You can do the walk of shame at any age.

We both quietly walked outside. My old pimp ride was sitting out in the driveway looking sad and helpless. My car just didn't quite fit into the environment. It was a beat-up Honda and every car that passed his place that morning was a Mercedes, BMW, or Range Rover, and I did see a Bentley go by.

L&D was in a rush to make his train into the city. Since Carlton wanted to walk a bit, I waved him on and said I would leave in a few minutes. We kissed goodbye and he was off to the train station.

I made my way back to my car, settled Carlton in the passenger seat, and put the key into the ignition. Nothing happened. Oh, my God! WTF? This can't be happening? I tried again and again and again, but nothing. The car was dead. I started to dial L&D because I knew he wouldn't be far. He didn't answer. Again I tried his number. No answer. After the eighth call without an answer, panic started to set in. I was in the middle of nowhere, no L&D, car dead as a door nail, battery dying on my cell phone, and a hungry dog in my passenger seat. What the hell was I going to do?

Finally, after the ninth call, L&D picked up and lo and behold, he was on the train already and acted as if he hadn't heard his phone. What I really wanted to say at that moment was, "Really, buddy? You didn't hear your phone? I wasn't born yesterday." He told me to knock on the door and wake his son up. Oh my God! This wasn't happening...are you kidding me? As I pounded on the front door, apparently L&D was also calling his son to wake him up. His son appeared at the door dazed, confused, and looking exactly like I did: hair matted, disheveled, and pissed off. I'm sure he wasn't happy his father had now put the responsibility on his shoulders to help me jump-start my car.

So just picture this scene: crappy, beat-up car in front of a nice home, me wearing my clothes from the night before, tight jeans, leopard-skin, three-inch-high-heeled crop boots, fake fur coat, little white dog shaking in the front seat, 25 degrees, my new beau's teenaged son on the phone with his dad getting a tutorial on how to jump start a car step by step. I wondered what was going through his mind and what he was thinking of me. I truly can't make this stuff up, this would only happen to me.

As luck had it, my pimp ride started up as soon as he clamped the cables to my car battery. We let the car run for a good twenty minutes. I thanked him profusely and off I went, back to the city, trying not to look back. At this point, I wondered if I should continue my relationship with L&D. He was not my type. I had no feelings for him at all. I had to end the relationship and this wasn't going to be easy. I decided to meet him for brunch one Sunday mid-morning in Evanston.

As we sat down, he said to me, "Notice anything different about me?"

Let's just say, I'm like a guy at times. Unless you drastically change something about yourself, I am oblivious and will not notice.

I said to him, "No. What's different about you?"

A look of disgust appeared on his face—his posture said it all—and he said, "What? You don't notice anything? Jenn, look at my hair. I dyed it. Don't you like it? I can't believe you didn't notice it."

At that point I should have cut my losses. I should have said goodbye to L&D a long time before. As I slightly nodded my head and said, "Yes, your hair looks fabulous," I was ready to deliver the bad news to him that I no longer wanted to see him.

tater tot nachos

TATER TOT NACHOS

YIELD: 4–6 SERVINGS

1 (32 oz. or larger) bag frozen
Tater Tots

16 oz. Velveeta cheese, small cubes

⅓ cup heavy cream

1 cup cooked, chopped, crisp bacon

⅓ cup green onions, chopped

1 cup cooked, warm, pulled pork

Bake Tater Tots according to package instructions and let them get very crisp and golden brown. In small saucepan, melt cubed Velveeta on low heat. Do not burn bottom. Stir often. Once cheese is melted, add in heavy cream. Stir and blend together. Take large dish and spread Tater Tots out. Sprinkle pulled pork over top of Tater Tots. Pour melted cheese over. Sprinkle bacon crumbles. Garnish with green onions. Serve immediately.

cotton candy martini

COTTON CANDY MARTINI

Ice

2–3 oz. cotton candy flavored vodka (Pinnacle)

½ cup Hawaiian blue fruit punch

cotton candy

1 packet Pop Rocks

⅓ cup honey

In cocktail shaker, add ice to ¾ of the way to the top. Pour in vodka and fruit punch. Shake vigorously for 10–15 seconds. Take two small plates and pour honey onto one plate. Add Pop Rocks to the other plate. Take martini glass and coat rim of glass with honey. After rim has been coated, roll rim of glass through Pop Rocks until entire rim is coated. Place small handful of cotton candy in bottom of glass. Pour vodka/punch mixture over cotton candy. Serve.

COTTON CANDY MARTINI

If you are wondering where to find cotton-candy-flavored vodka, try a large liquor store in your area that offers more of a selection. Pinnacle makes a great cotton-candy flavor.

If you cannot find cotton-candy vodka, try the following in place of it: 1 oz. of vanilla vodka and 2 oz. of cherry or raspberry vodka.

Chapter 3

Friends

Guava-Barbeque Glazed Chicken

Coconut Basmati Rice

Pineapple, Mango, Spam, and Serrano Salsa

Pineapple, Papaya, Citrus Vinaigrette

Knock-Your-Knees-Off Potato Salad

Fried Coconut Shrimp with Watermelon and Jicama Coleslaw

Steak Bites with Bloody Mary Sauce

Veal Osso Bucco with Gremolata

Mushroom-Leek Risotto

Whole Wheat Penne with Spicy Puttanesca Sauce and Mussels

Citrus-Herb Salmon

Ray's Famous Chopped Medley Salad

Fresh-off-the-Boat, Seared Coriander-Cilantro Ahi Tuna with Citrus-Wasabi Glaze

Black Bean, Corn, and Roasted Red Pepper Salad, Topped with Lime-Tequila Grilled Shrimp

Matambritos de Chancho and Pico de Gallo (Argentine Flank Steak with Chimichurri)

Grilled Fruit over Angel Food Cake with Sangria Sauce

Kenny's Famous Sangria

The glory of friendship is not the outstretched hand, nor the kindly smile, nor the joy of companionship; it is the spiritual inspiration that comes to one when you discover that someone else believes in you and is willing to trust you with a friendship.

—Ralph Waldo Emerson

You meet a myriad people in your life and only a few of them you call your friends. I have been lucky to have such amazing friends—and such amazing food memories to go with them. All of these people I am writing about have affected my life in so many ways. I could not have achieved my dreams and aspirations without them and I am truly blessed to have them as part of my life.

Megan, Kelly, and...

Guava-Barbeque Glazed Chicken

Coconut Basmati Rice

Pineapple, Mango, Spam, and Serrano Salsa

Pineapple-Papaya Citrus Vinaigrette

My recipes for guava-barbeque glazed chicken with pineapple, mango, Spam, and serrano salsa, field greens with a pineapple-papaya citrus dressing and coconut basmati rice were created on the island of Oahu. It was December 2006 and my best friends from Kansas City and I were all meeting in Honolulu to run the biggest race of our lives, a full-fledged marathon. It would be my first marathon and what better place to run your first marathon than Hawaii, right? Well, what I was really thinking was what the hell I was getting myself into.

As we landed in Honolulu and tried to settle in before the marathon, we all had such nervous energy that we couldn't sleep the night before the big. I was up every hour on the hour and when 3:00 a.m. hit, I was exhausted and marathon day was here. The house we were renting was nestled high up on a massive hill (probably some sort of volcano) in a quaint cul-de-sac in a residential area of Honolulu. The house was church-quiet that morning. I could smell fresh Kona coffee brewing, hear ocean waves off in the distance, and smell the medicated muscle spray filtrating the hallway. We all were dressed with our best marathon attire: bib numbers pinned to our Dri-FIT shirts, chip tags securely looped through our shoe laces, and our iPods in their waterproof/sweat-proof cases, wrapped around our arms. From the night before, we all were stuffed from the massive amount of pasta we had eaten, but we managed to wash down a banana and bagel. I think we were the poster kids for carb-loading. We piled in our official race van (high-end minivan) and sped off toward the starting line to endure the biggest challenge of our lives. I thought, if I can finish this race, 26.2 miles, I can do anything in my life for years to come. Brad dropped us off at the closest spot to the starting line. The massive numbers of people wandering around in so many directions made me feel as if I were at a baseball game that was in the ninth inning, home team losing, and everyone was trying to run to their cars to beat the traffic. It was 4:30 a.m. The sun was nowhere in sight as we made our way to the starting corrals where the National Anthem was to be sung. Nervous energy was filling up my entire body and I had second thoughts about running the race. There was no turning back at this point. When the gun shot sounded, a man's voice over the PA system wished everyone good luck and we all moved forward. I said to Kelly and Megan, "Let's go FSSU!" (Translation: fuck some shit up!)

We all ran our little hearts out and I finished the race in five hours and six minutes. It was the most challenging thing I have ever done in my life and I am alive to tell the story. And what better place to recover than Hawaii.

After we all crossed the finish line and lived to tell about it, we made our way to the race van that was parked a half mile away. We were in so much pain we walked like ninety-five-year-old women with Depends on. Everything on our bodies hurt, down to our toe nails. We spotted the van off in the distance, and I was relieved that we would soon be sitting. We all piled our stinky, sweaty, filthy bodies into the van and headed back to the house. On the main highway in Honolulu, traffic came to a complete stop. Some of the roads were still closed because of the marathon, so the highway was a parking lot. We were ten minutes from our rental house and I really had to go to the bathroom. The water that I had retained from the race was ready to be released and if I didn't get to a restroom in the next ten minutes, I was going to have an accident all over our official race van.

"We should be back at the house within fifteen minutes," Brad yelled from the driver's seat. He was my girlfriend Kelly's fiancé.

Okay. That was good. I could hold out.

The pain grew more intense and I had to go. There were cars on all sides of us and we were not moving. I was in a panic because we couldn't move and our car was trapped. I had to go and I had to think quickly about what I was going to do. The pain had reached an all-time high and I was almost in tears. I turned to Megan and Kelly and asked them to hold towels up around me. I had no choice at this moment.

I took my two sports bottles from the marathon, dumped the Gatorade out the window, and said to Megan, "I'm going for it. Hold up these towels."

With everyone in the van cringing and trying not to think about what I was doing, I tried to aim the best I could into the small opening of the sports bottle. Thank God I had emptied the second sports bottle because I was filling up the first one fast. It was that exact scene from the movie *Dumb and Dumber* in which Jim Carey in the sheep-dog truck pees in beer bottles and has to switch to another empty bottle mid-stream. With a little spillage on the van floor, I achieved success. I was no longer in pain. This was not my proudest moment, but I was extremely relieved.

As we pulled up to our vacation bungalow, we all realized that we had over a hundred steps to climb to gain access to our rental house.

"Oh my God, there is no way in hell I can walk up those stone steps. I can't even feel my legs. I can't walk," Megan said in sheer exhaustion.

Single file, we all made our way up the steps, and for every step we took, each of us let out a deep groan. You would have thought a porno film was being shot. All of us were moving very slowly up the steps, one step at a time like three little toddlers learning to walk for the first time. As we crested the last step, I remembered I had to go back down to the race van and clean up aftermath of the sports bottle spillage.

Our rental house was on a mountain side, overlooking the ocean in a tightly knit community. It was a tranquil, breath-taking view, and every morning we had our routine down. We all got up before sunrise because our bodies couldn't adjust to the time difference. We grabbed the Lucky Charms, milk, bowls, spoons, and coffee, and had breakfast on the patio watching the sunrise with the sounds of native singer IZ playing in the background.

On the last night of our trip, we invited a few of Megan's local friends over to the house. They were transplants from the United States. For our last night together, I wanted to prepare an authentic

Hawaiian meal for everyone. I wanted to use a lot of the local, indigenous ingredients that Hawaii had to offer. Megan and I hopped into the speedy race van and went to a local market to see what Pacific Rim ingredients we could find. I had no idea what I was going to cook for everyone, but I knew which ingredients I wanted. I felt as if Megan and I were on the *Amazing Race* and *Iron Chef* competitions. We were running through a small grocery store just grabbing ingredients that looked as if they would work for our Hawaiian meal. Megan was across the store yelling, "What about this ingredient? This looks good."

I told her, "Throw it in, my friend. We'll find a use for it."

The ingredients in the market were out of this world. Fruits I had never seen before were bursting with vibrant colors and sweet citrus smells. There were various sizes and colors of rice noodle, bizarre-looking fish species, and an endless supply of Spam products. A lot of the produce items were the same that we used on the main land, but there were some peculiar little specimens amongst the selection that looked as if they were from another planet. There were endless ingredients to choose from and my creative juices were on overdrive. On the ride home, the menu came to life and lo and behold, this was created: guava-barbeque glazed chicken with pineapple, mango, Spam, and serrano salsa, coconut basmati rice, orange-juice-pickled red onions, and field greens with pineapple-papaya citrus vinaigrette.

As the masterpiece came together, my sous chefs ,Megan and Kelly, were taking the last of the guava-barbeque chicken off the grill. It looked outstanding. A nice caramelized, crisp, dark-charred crust had formed on the outside of the chicken from the sugars in the guava and barbeque sauce. The large, round table on the patio was set with little white tea candles, beautiful Hawaiian flowers for the center piece, and the glowing light from the candles made the wine glasses sparkle like stars in the solar system. It was a picturesque scene. It looked very intimate with the sun setting over the ocean. Brad was on party patrol, which meant everyone had to have a full glass of libation at all times and the rocking music never stopped. Dinner lasted a few hours. We all reminisced about the race and talked about our Kansas City memories, and of course about the food. The party turned out very well, and I was just happy to cook for everyone on our last night.

As we continued our gastronomical evening on the patio, sipping our pineapple-guava martinis with full tummies, Megan, Kelly, and I noticed a bug scurry swiftly across the patio. We all screamed and it disappeared through the cracks of the warped, wooden boards. That little bugger was gone, whatever it was. Our conversation continued until all of sudden the same bug flew toward us. We jumped up, screamed, and ran inside the house in the hope that this flying rodent wasn't on one of us. Even the manly men of the group were freaked out by this thing.

It was giant flying cockroach the size of a large mouse. Apparently, according to the local ladies, these little creatures are very prevalent on the islands. All the girls hid inside screaming as the four guys set out to find this mammoth thing. It surfaced somehow inside the house. It was like a scene from a scary movie when the helpless girl is alone in the house and the killer is right behind her and she has no idea that he's there, ready to strike. This creepy creature was ready to strike because it crawled across the wall inside the house, and all of us girls were standing in front of the thing with no idea it was behind us.

The boys were outside on the porch with flashlights looking into all the cracks and crevasses when suddenly Brad yelled from the porch, "Behind you!"

All hell broke loose. Screaming at the top of our lungs, we were trying to move as fast as we could away from this monster, when it flew toward us and landed on the floor. We all made it outside. The little varmint didn't survive to see the next day. The guys ran in and crushed it to death. What a mess that was.

I turned to Brad and said, "Hey, party patrol, I think everyone is going to need some more drinks."

The meal Jennifer created in Hawaii set the mood for one of my most memorable evenings. Completing the Honolulu marathon was truly the most difficult experience of my life, and I felt so fortunate to celebrate such a huge accomplishment with close friends. Sitting on the lanai, enjoying the fabulous Hawaiian sunset, and eating a delicious meal were the perfect reward. Jennifer's use of fresh ingredients, such as mango, coconut, and pineapple, truly captured the essence of Hawaii. The best thing about her recipes was that we could re-create them easily at home. Now, every time I feel nostalgic for Hawaii, I simply fire up one of Jennifer's recipes and my husband and I are instantly transported back.

—Kelly Papa

guava-barbeque glazed chicken

GUAVA-BARBEQUE GLAZED CHICKEN
YIELD: 4–6 SERVINGS

⅔ cup guava paste or jam (try Goya brand)

1¼ cup barbeque sauce

½ cup chicken stock

¼ teaspoon pepper

½ teaspoon salt

4-6 chicken breasts, boneless, skinless

Put chicken breasts in baking dish. Season with salt and pepper on both sides. Set aside in fridge.

In saucepan, add guava paste/jam, barbeque sauce, chicken stock, salt, and pepper. Bring to boil. Whisk sauce until all guava paste is dissolved. Turn down to low heat and cook for 15–20 minutes.

Brush chicken breast with barbeque sauce mixture. Grill chicken and baste with sauce throughout grilling process.

SCORE TIP:

GUAVA-BARBEQUE GLAZED CHICKEN

Guava paste consists of guava pulp, pectin, sugar, and some form of citric acid. It is slowly cooked until it becomes an extremely thick paste. You can usually find this product in the Latin section of your local grocery stores. If you can't find guava paste, you can use guava jam.

COCONUT BASMATI RICE

2 cups basmati rice

1 tablespoon olive oil

⅓ cup green onions, chopped

¼ teaspoon garlic, minced

1½ cups coconut milk

¼ cup white wine

2 cups chicken stock

salt and pepper

In saucepan, heat coconut milk, wine, and chicken stock to boil. Lower heat and allow to simmer, cover with lid. In medium saucepan, heat olive oil. Add garlic and green onions. Cook for 3-4 minutes on medium heat. Add rice and cook until rice is slightly toasted. Add stock mixture, ½-¾ cup at a time, stirring constantly. Allow rice to absorb liquid before adding more broth. Keep doing this until rice becomes al dente—approximately 20-22 minutes. Season with salt and pepper.

PINEAPPLE, MANGO, SPAM, AND SERRANO SALSA

YIELD: 6–8 SERVINGS

1 whole pineapple, peeled, core removed, diced small

1 mango, peeled, diced small

1 serrano pepper, seeds and white pith removed, diced small

1 small red onion, diced small

1⅓ cups Spam, seared and diced small

1 tablespoon chopped jalapeño, seeds and white pith removed

⅓ cup fresh cilantro, chopped

¼ cup apple cider vinegar

2 tablespoons olive oil

½ teaspoon cracked pepper

1 teaspoon cumin

½ teaspoon salt

Heat medium sauté pan with a little olive oil on high. Put loaf of Spam in center of pan and sear until both sides are crisp and golden brown. Remove from pan, cool on plate, and cut into small cubes. Mix all ingredients together in a medium-sized bowl. Mix until all is incorporated. Refrigerate for several hours.

PINEAPPLE-PAPAYA CITRUS VINAIGRETTE

YIELD: 4–6 SERVINGS

¼ cup pineapple juice

¼ cup fresh papaya juice

2 tablespoons apple cider vinegar

1 teaspoon lemon juice

1 teaspoon yellow mustard

2 teaspoons honey

½ cup olive oil

¼ teaspoon salt

⅛ teaspoon black ground pepper

field greens or mesclun mix

In small bowl, add all ingredients except olive oil. Whisk to combine. Slowly drizzle in olive oil, whisking back and forth until all olive oil is gone and all ingredients come together.

Serve over field greens.

CAROLINA AND...

CAROLINA AND...

KNOCK-YOUR-KNEES-OFF POTATO SALAD

Where do I begin with this amusing story? The name alone makes me laugh. I guess you can say this is an inside joke between my best friend, Carolina, and myself. As I mentioned in the beginning, if it had not been for her dedication and her drive to push me to the limit, this cookbook would have never happened. As fate would have it, I had been praying to meet a best friend like Carolina for a long time. A girl just has to have that one special person to be her friend for life, no matter what happens.

When I met Carolina, I was working with one of my accounts in New Mexico. Carolina was the marketing manager for this account and had only been working there for a few months. We bonded immediately and the rest is history. We acquired that special friendship, a friendship that only comes around once in a blue moon.

After I left New Mexico, our friendship flourished. We were instant BFFs. Carolina decided to head up to Connecticut for a fun-filled weekend with me. Being a native Brazilian, this was her first time coming up to the Northeast. Being so close to New York City, the second night of her visit we decided to head into the city to go out with my friend, Jerry. I know what you're thinking: She was in for a big treat with Jerry. This is the same guy mentioned in the "Brad" story, who did the cartwheel in his Superman under-roos at my ex's parents' house, hit the wall in his drunken state, landed on the floor, and was found by my ex's mother. She was in for a fun-filled night and what better night to have fun in Manhattan than Halloween night? We were ready to paint the town red. We stepped out onto 51st Street and the sea

of fictitious characters in their elaborate costumes engulfed us as they walked around like actors on a Paramount Studio lot waiting for their shining moment on camera.

The drinks didn't stop all night. Carolina was mildly overwhelmed but having fun. Jerry wanted to take us to his favorite local hang out, a place called Therapy—catchy name for a bar.

"Where are you going tonight?"

"Oh, just going to Therapy."

It was a sexy tavern filled with men. I was in paradise.

"Wow! There are all men here and really no women," I said to Carolina. For sure, I would be winning a few digits tonight.

Jerry handed me a drink with a smirk on his face and said, "Jenn, we're in a gay bar. So no offense, but they're going to want my number."

As we closed down Therapy, and Jerry showed us his trophy digits, we jumped onto the subway to head back to Jerry's apartment. We all seemed to be feeling no pain. The subway was semi-crowded with the aftermath of the Halloween creatures. Jerry and I decided to start singing old sitcom songs. Carolina froze as our battered voices tried to carry on the tune to *Facts of Life*. Our stop arrived. We stumbled off the subway, laughing, as the crowd pulling away stared at us. Our short walk home seemed like a marathon distance.

All of sudden Jerry yelled, "Round number two!"

With my mind in a drunken state, I had no idea what he was talking about. In the mere seconds it took for him to announce this, I saw him out of the corner of my eye start a cartwheel, and it didn't go well this time either. A massive thud echoed down the busy Manhattan street and Jerry lay motionless in the middle of the sidewalk.

Carolina and I immediately started yelling, "Jerry, are you okay?"

After five seconds, he started laughing. We helped him up and headed toward his apartment to call it a night.

As we tried to recover the next morning from the mango-cardamom martinis, shots of tequila, and near-fatal cartwheel accidents, we had to muster up enough strength for Kenny's Oktoberfest party that night, back in Connecticut. We stumbled out onto the Manhattan streets feeling like vampires seeing sunlight for the first time. I was grateful my car was still in the parking lot where I had left it. We grabbed our Starbucks coffees and drove back to Connecticut. I called Kenny and told him I would make a potato salad, and because I'm a chef, you know that I can't just make a plain, old potato salad. We finally made it back to my townhouse. Carolina was still nursing her hangover. She plopped on the couch as I whipped up the knock-your-knees-off potato salad.

As we headed over to the party, I brought Carolina up to speed on the type of people we would be hanging with. It was going to be completely different from our NYC outing. Some of my friends were twenty plus years older than I was and the complete opposite of my crazy, zany friends. You could say they were more set in their ways and not too much into the partying scene. Carolina and I arrived at Kenny's house around six-thirtyish, with the knock-your-knees-off potato salad and Peronis in hand. I introduced the

brazen Brazilian to the crowd of partygoers. The sounds of Simon and Garfunkel filled the house on top of the various conversations. Needless to say, we were ready for some stronger cocktails to liven us and the party up.

Since Kenny's event was an Oktoberfest party, our only options were a round-the-world selection of beers. Not being a big beer fan, I had brought an emergency stash of vodka and mixers. We didn't want to share our alcoholic concoctions with the rest of the patrons because we didn't have enough to go around, so we went into Kenny's bathroom to mix our cocktails. Carolina and I were laughing so hard— we felt like sixteen-year-olds at our parents' house, sneaking alcohol. We were grown adults mixing alcoholic beverages in a bathroom. What is wrong with this picture?

As we opened the bathroom door with our bright red pomegranate cocktails in hand, we really didn't care what everyone thought at this point. We were on a mission. As our delightful Oktoberfest dinner was served, the knock–your-knees-off potato salad was well received. We washed down a few brats with our pomegranate cocktail coolers and we felt no pain. As the night progressed, so did our decibel level. Carolina and I were in our own little world, sitting on an ottoman near the kitchen, trying to entertain one another. A lot of my friends were sitting around the kitchen table talking about current events and finishing up their desserts. We were on our third "liquid dessert" and laughing about our zany night in NYC, with plenty of disapproving stares from all the party goers as I tried to sing the *Facts of Life* tune to Carolina again.

Kenny's party was moving at a slow pace with quiet conversations about never-ending ailments and future vacations. Carolina and I started playing a game of hand slap (yes, we are grown adults). I rested my two hands on hers and I overly dramatized the pull-back motion of my hands so

Carolina could not slap them. As I jerked my arms back, I fell backward onto the floor, knocking over my bright red cocktail with my entire body. All I could do was lie on the floor laughing and looking at the huge bright red pomegranate stain I had left on Kenny's white carpet. Carolina covered her mouth in shock and started laughing. Everyone looked at the two of us and shook their heads, just as my parents would have done if I'd done something wrong in front of the family. Kenny was hysterical and immediately got out his carpet cleaning kit. The stain came out, but it was time for Carolina and I to depart. We left a not-so-pleasant memory among the crowd, but everyone who was at the party will remember that knock-your-knees-off potato salad—I hope.

KNOCK-YOUR-KNEES-OFF POTATO SALAD

YIELD: 4–6 SERVINGS

2 lb. red-skinned potatoes

1 tablespoon balsamic vinegar

½ cup mayonnaise

¼ cup sour cream

1 tablespoon fresh chives, chopped

1 tablespoon fresh mint leaves, chopped

1 tablespoon fresh parsley, chopped

1 tablespoon honey

½ lemon, squeezed

½ teaspoon hot sauce

salt and pepper

GARNISH

smoked sea salt (optional)

In large pot, place potatoes, salt, and water. Bring to boil and cook until potatoes are tender. Strain and cool. Once potatoes are cooled, cut into bite-sized chunks and set aside.

In small bowl, place vinegar, mayonnaise, sour cream, chives, mint, parsley, honey, lemon juice, and hot sauce. Whisk and blend all together. Season with salt and pepper to taste.

In large bowl, place potatoes and pour dressing over top. Blend until potatoes are coated. Put in fridge for several hours before serving. Garnish with smoked sea salt (optional).

SCORE TIP:

KNOCK-YOUR-KNEES-OFF POTATO SALAD

Over the last few years, various types of gourmet salts have been hitting the scene and making a huge statement. You can find these salts just about anywhere. From Hawaiian pink salt and black lava salt to flavored salts, they really add a special touch to your dishes. With the wide variety of salts on the market today, you can learn how to utilize them in your very own dishes. You will be able to taste the way salt enhances the flavor and finish of all your foods. In this recipe, I garnish the potato salad with smoked salt.

Smoked sea salt: this is my favorite enhancing salt. It's best used to finish a dish, just as I did in the potato salad recipe. The smell of this salt when I first open the bottle brings me back to a chilly fall night sitting around a campfire. When buying a smoked salt, make sure that it is naturally smoked and doesn't have a liquid smoked flavoring added to it, which can create a very bitter taste. Salts that are smoked naturally in cold smokers for a long period have time to infuse the smoke of the wood and create an unbelievable taste.

Italian sea salt: this is produced along the coast of Sicily. It is a natural salt rich in minerals, including fluorine, iodine, magnesium, and potassium, with a slightly lower percentage of sodium than regular table salt. This type of salt is very delicate in taste and is a great finishing salt because it is not overpowering like regular table salt. It's best used on roasts, pastas, salads, pizza, and fresh tomatoes.

Hawaiian sea salt: this earthy, mellow salt is a great finishing salt. Its gorgeous color is obtained from a natural mineral called alae, a volcanic, baked, red clay. It is added to enrich the salt with iron oxide. This salt is a staple ingredient among Hawaiians and is a great salt to use on roasted pig, prime rib, and my guava-barbequeued chicken dish.

Keith and...

Fried Coconut Shrimp
with Watermelon and Jicama Coleslaw

It was a cold day in February, and I was halfway through my Restaurant Teaching Assistant/Sous Chef fellowship at the CIA. On this particular day, everything was spiraling out of control. If one thing went wrong, five more things followed right behind. It was Valentine's night and we had a packed house in the restaurant. My students were screwing up every dish, numerous complaints were coming in from the customers, the servers were uncooperative and unruly, the food looked terrible, the tickets wouldn't stop coming in, and the executive chef and I were in a shouting match the entire night. I couldn't wait until the night was over. Oh, did I mention that my executive chef/instructor and I had a mini fling going for a while and this was the night it ended? Lovely!

The kitchen, when service was over, looked as if an M80 had gone off and blown it to pieces. The students, servers, and I had a few hours to pick up the pieces and put the restaurant back to normal. I finished up all my paperwork, placed my food order for the next day, and made my final notes on inventory while the busy little bees were just about finished cleaning the kitchen. I packed up my stuff, dismissed the class, and headed home. The whole ride back I cried because I was so upset and burned out. I wanted to quit and throw my whole career away. I prayed for a miracle to get me out of this horrible night.

I finally arrived home and sat down at my computer desk with my chef coat on, smelling like burned toast, roasted garlic, seared steak, and chocolate cake. I was looking over some personal emails when my cell phone rang. Who the hell was calling me at that hour? I answered the phone and heard a voice I hadn't heard in a long time. It belonged to the buddy I worked with in Kansas City, Keith.

"Hey stranger," I said. "I haven't talked to you since I left KC."

He'd only been on the phone for thirty seconds when he said, "Girl, I have been trying to get a hold of you. Don't you check your e-mail?"

I told him I rarely checked that account and was very interested in what he was so eager to talk to me about. He told me he had the opportunity of a lifetime for me—something I couldn't refuse. He wanted me to costar in a pilot cooking show with one of his good buddies who would be the star of the show. David was going to direct and produce the show for his friend and thought I would be the perfect candidate for the job. I thought he was kidding. Was this my big break? I had wished for a miracle that night and it came true.

Within a week, I flew out to Denver for the pilot shoot. When I arrived at the airport, Keith Jones, the host of the show, greeted me with open arms. Keith Jones, aka the Champagne Chef, was an off-the-wall, dynamic, crazy chef who wore these in-your-face chef clothes. Meeting for the first time, there was instant chemistry between us. We shared a high-energy, charismatic, full-of-life personality and it was an on-camera match made in heaven. This whole experience was so surreal; I still couldn't believe that it was happening to me.

Keith took me to where the pilot was going to be shot. I met the two producers, production crew, and executive producer. I started to get very nervous because this was the real deal; it was finally sinking in. As we started to go over the grueling production schedule, I heard a few familiar voices enter the room—David and TJ, my old film buddies from Kansas City. I was ecstatic to see them. These were the two who had brought this harmonious match together.

While I was there, I also met Andre Ward, who would be the *Emeril*-type band in all of our episodes. He was a one-man show and would be our musician side-kick in the pilot, kind of like Paul Shaffer on *Late Show with David Letterman*.

When the day ended, I went back to the hotel room to prepare for the biggest event of my life. I tried to memorize my lines, but I knew I would be adlibbing a lot and feeding off Keith's energy. I couldn't sleep that night, knowing that I would be filming a cooking show series pilot. The morning came early and we all met down in the lobby to be picked up and shuttled to the film set. When we arrived, I was escorted to the make-up and wardrobe room where I met James. He was the genius and artist behind my hair, make-up, and wardrobe. James was ¾ done when the executive producer's assistant came into the make-up room with her head-set and clip board ready to take me to set to start taping the first episode. My stomach was in knots and I felt as if I was going to throw up at any minute.

She clicked her little button on her walkie-talkie headset and said, "She'll need ten more minutes and then I'll bring her to the set."

I heard a man's deep voice in her head-phones say, "Okay, hurry it up."

The director gave us the rundown of the first episode and told us what we needed to do and say. When the director called out, "Action!" on the very first take, I shouted my opening lines at the top of my lungs, "Introducing the Champagne Chef!" Up went my hand as if I were a model on *The Price is Right*, displaying a new car to the audience. Andre Ward started wailing away on his saxophone as if he were making hot passionate love, playing the opening theme of the show. Out came Keith Jones, clapping and full of energy as if he had just downed a case of Red Bull. He performed as if he were in front of a massive studio audience although his audience was just the camera guys, floor producers, sound guys, and director. I had my pretty little dress on. My make-up was flawless. My hair was coiffed to perfection and I wore a black apron ready to get my hands dirty. The first episode was a little rocky because we were trying to get the dynamics and flow down. After my eighth time saying, "Introducing the Champagne Chef," I was ready to get this show on the road. We had twelve more episodes to tape in only two days.

Filming on such a tight schedule was difficult, grueling, and tiring, but I didn't mind because I was in my glory. I had never had such an amazing, mind-blowing experience. When the director yelled, "Cut!" on our last episode, the whole crew and cast started clapping and cheering with sheer joy. The producers wanted us to head outside and take a final photograph of the group. I remember the sun was setting into the beautiful Denver mountains, the most peaceful, amazing sunset I had ever seen.

I said to myself, "My dream is becoming a reality. It has just begun. Look out world, here comes Chef Jenn Stoker."

SCORE TIP:

FRIED COCONUT SHRIMP WITH WATERMELON AND JICAMA SALSA

Jicama is part of the legume family and is a staple in Latin America. The popularity of Latin cuisine in the past few years has brought this amazing vegetable onto the culinary scene. If you have never seen a jicama, it resembles a huge turnip or radish. It's usually eaten raw and it's best used in salads, salsas, and raw veggie platters. I really like to use jicama in a lot of my salads because of the crunchy texture and mildly sweet taste. If I had to describe the taste, I'd say it's a cross between a crunchy water chestnut and mild green apple.

If by chance you can't find jicama in your grocery store, you can replace it with whole water chestnuts, chopped, or you could use a peeled green apple if you want to add more sweetness.

fried coconut shrimp with watermelon and jicama coleslaw

FRIED COCONUT SHRIMP WITH WATERMELON AND JICAMA COLESLAW

YIELD: 6–8 SERVINGS

24 jumbo shrimp, peeled, deveined and tails left on

½ cup corn starch

¾ teaspoon salt

¼ teaspoon pepper

2¼ cups sweetened, shredded coconut

1 teaspoon ginger, finely chopped

¼ teaspoon red chili flakes

4 large egg whites

vegetable oil (for frying)

In medium bowl, mix together corn starch, salt, and pepper. In shallow dish, mix together coconut, ginger, and chili flakes. In another medium bowl, whisk together egg whites until light and frothy. Dredge shrimp in cornstarch mixture; shake off excess. Dip into egg white mixture. Dip shrimp into coconut mixture, making sure all sides of shrimp are coated. Place on plate. Repeat until all shrimp is done. Place in freezer for 20 minutes.

In large saucepan, fill with oil to about 2 inches high. Heat oil to 365 degrees. Take a plate and line with paper towels and have slotted spoon ready.

Work in batches to ensure oil temp does not drop. Cook shrimp for 2–3 minutes until shrimp is thoroughly cooked and golden brown. Drain on paper towel and season with salt. Repeat until all shrimp are fried. Serve with watermelon and jicama salsa.

WATERMELON AND JICAMA COLESLAW

1 small miniature watermelon, seed removed and diced small

1 medium Jicama, skin peeled, diced small

⅓ cup green onions, chopped

1 tablespoon chives, chopped

½ cup red onion, chopped

⅓ cup feta cheese crumbles

2 tablespoons olive oil

1 tablespoon balsamic vinegar

½ lemon, squeezed

salt and pepper

In medium bowl, add all ingredients and toss together until all ingredients are blended. Season with salt and pepper. Refrigerate for several hours before serving with coconut shrimp.

Christina and...
Steak Bites with Bloody Mary Sauce
Veal Osso Bucco with Gremolata
Mushroom-Leek Risotto

I first met Christina when I started culinary school at the CIA. We were in our first six weeks of lectures when I introduced myself to her in our culinary math class. I knew we were going to be great friends for a long time. She was fresh out of high school, New Jersey-born, high Red Bull energy level, and heart of gold. During the first six months of school, almost the whole class became inseparable. I had never had such a bond with a group of people and I felt as if we were all family. After we survived culinary school, Christina landed a prestigious job at the Waldorf Astoria hotel. We were only a few hours away from one another, and our friendship never skipped a beat.

On a very chilly day in December, I called Christina on her one day off from the Waldorf and asked her if she could be my sous chef for a private dinner party I was hired to cater. The host was a gentleman who worked for my company, and he wanted to give his wife something very special for Christmas. He decided to hire me to cook an elaborate four-course dinner at their home. Christina agreed, packed her knives, and made her way to Connecticut.

On the day of the party, we arrived a little early. We were greeted with a warm welcome by Mr. Sanborn, who helped us unload my car, jam-packed with food and cooking equipment. As we made our way through his house, we noticed it was dimly lit. Candles were burning in every space. Rose petals were scattered on every surface, and the sounds of light jazz filled the room. Wow! He was the most romantic guy on the planet. His wife was in for a big surprise. Why couldn't I meet a guy like that?

We set up shop in the kitchen and started preparing their meal. Christina organized the kitchen to ease the flow of the night's work and avoid chaos, while I started marinating the meat for the Bloody Mary steak bites. The sauce was already made for the steak bites; we just had to heat it up. The risotto rice had to be toasted to create a nutty flavor and bring out more of the creaminess that characterizes a risotto dish.

The night was about to begin. Christina retrieved the happy couple from their sitting room and escorted them to their dining room table. I presented them with menus and explained each course in detail. The courses went flawlessly. The scallop "sandwich" was brushed with a light citrus sauce before it left the sauté pan and was placed between two thin cucumber slices with crisp water chestnuts topped with sun-dried tomato chutney and crisp curry shallots. The Bloody Mary steak bites were cooked to a medium-rare consistency, the sauce being ever so slightly spicy with a bit of a tang to finish it. With every course, I paired a fantastic wine. We maintained the five-star dining experience throughout the evening and every time Christina went back and cleared their dishes to get ready for the next course, they had no complaints. For the finale, I presented the dessert: an elegant display of three homemade sorbets paired with a nice shot of ice-cold Limoncello. If you have never had Limoncello before, it's like drinking ice-cold, lemon jet fuel.

After Christina and I finished cleaning up, the happy couple was nowhere to be found. They had left the dining-room table. We thought they might have stepped out to have a cigarette. When we finished packing up the car, I called out into the dark, barren house that we were leaving. Then I heard moans as if a porno movie were being filmed in the next room.

The husband called out, "Thanks, Chef Jennifer. Everything was very delicious. I left you a check on the front table."

So, I just looked at Christina and said, "Well, I know there is a lot of love and passion in my food, but this definitely proves it."

steak bites with bloody mary sauce

STEAK BITES WITH BLOODY MARY SAUCE
YIELD: 4 SERVINGS

1½ – 2 lb. stewing beef cubes

2 cups spicy vegetable juice

¼ cup olive oil

1 tablespoon Worcestershire sauce

1 teaspoon salt

½ teaspoon cracked pepper

BLOODY MARY SAUCE

2 tablespoons olive oil

1 teaspoon garlic, chopped

⅓ cup green onions, chopped

⅓ cup vodka

2½ cups spicy vegetable juice

1 teaspoon Worcestershire sauce

¼ teaspoon red pepper flakes

wooden skewers

In large bowl, place chunks of beef, vegetable juice, olive oil, Worcestershire sauce, salt, and pepper. Mix together and make sure all beef is coated. Marinate for 12–24 hours.

To make sauce: heat 2 tablespoons olive oil in saucepan on medium-high. Add garlic and green onions. Cook for 3–4 minutes. Deglaze pan with vodka. Let liquid dissipate and cook for 4–6 minutes.

Add rest of vegetable juice, Worcestershire sauce, and pepper flakes. Bring to boil. Then reduce heat to simmer. Reduce sauce by ½. Add salt and pepper.

Soak all wooden skewers in water for 15– 20 minutes.

Put 4 pieces of meat onto each skewer. If using a grill, place on grill at 365 degrees and cook until desired doneness. If cooking in oven, place skewers on a baking sheet, side by side, and cook at 365 degrees until desired doneness. Serve with hot Bloody Mary sauce.

SCORE TIP:

STEAK BITES WITH BLOODY MARY SAUCE

If you have a gorgeous grill out on your deck, kick it up a gear and grill your Bloody Mary steak bites.

First things first, so you don't set your deck on fire, soak your wooden skewers in water for a good 20 –25 minutes. Heat your grill to 365 degrees, spear marinated meat on wooden skewers, and place on grill. Cook until desired consistency. I highly recommend a medium-rare to medium consistency for this recipe. You will thank me later.

VEAL OSSO BUCCO WITH GREMOLATA
YIELD: 4 SERVINGS

4 veal shanks

salt and pepper

½ cup flour

2 tablespoons olive oil

¼ cup green onions, chopped

2 teaspoons garlic, chopped

⅔ cup carrots, chopped

½ cup celery, chopped

1 cup yellow onions, chopped

2 tablespoons tomato paste

1 quart beef stock

1 cup red wine

¼ cup water

Preheat oven to 325 degrees.

Pat dry each veal shank with paper towels to remove any excess moisture. Veal shanks will brown better when they are dry. Season osso bucco shanks with salt and pepper. Dredge in flour and shake off excess.

In medium stockpot, heat olive oil until pan is smoking. Add shanks and sear top and bottom until a golden brown crust forms on both sides. Remove shanks from pot and let rest on a plate. Add carrots, celery, and onions to pot, stirring up the bits from the meat. Cook for 5–6 minutes. Add tomato paste and incorporate. Cook for another 2–3 minutes. Add wine and beef stock. Stir until all ingredients come together. Add veal back into pot. Liquid should cover ¾ of the meat. Bring to boil on stove top. Then cover with lid or foil and put in oven for 2–2½ hours.

Meat should be very tender and fall off the bone. Remove shanks carefully, keeping the meat on the bone. Set aside in baking dish and keep warm. Take braising liquid in pot and bring to a rolling boil. Reduce sauce to 1½ cups. Strain sauce. Top each veal shank with sauce.

GREMOLATA

½ cup fresh parsley, chopped

¼ cup lemon zest

1 tablespoon garlic, chopped

Mix together all ingredients in small bowl. Salt and pepper to taste. Top each veal osso bucco with a few pinches.

VEAL OSSO BUCCO

Osso bucco translates as "hollow bone" and refers to the hollow bone that holds the marrow of a veal shank. What makes the dish so rich and delicious is the cooking process. Low and slow, baby, that's how this meat likes it—low oven temperature and long cook time. This process breaks down the connective tissue throughout the meat and melts the marrow into the braising liquid to create a tasty, rich sauce and meat that falls off the bone. The veal shank is relatively inexpensive and is readily available at your local grocery store. The best dish to pair with osso bucco is a rich, creamy risotto. Traditionally, a very fragrant gremolata is sprinkled on top. This is a mixture of fresh lemon zest, garlic, and parsley that really blends all the flavors together and adds a nice zing to the dish.

mushroom-leek risotto

MUSHROOM-LEEK RISOTTO

YIELD: 4 SERVINGS

2 tablespoons olive oil

1 teaspoon garlic, minced

⅓ cup yellow onion, diced small

½ cup leeks, finely chopped

¼ cup green onions chopped

2½ cups of white mushrooms and cremini mushrooms, stems removed, chopped

1 pound risotto rice (Arborio or Carniola)

1½ quarts hot chicken stock, as needed

¼ cup water

½ cup white wine, as needed

⅓ cup Parmesan cheese

2 tablespoons butter

salt and pepper to taste

GARNISH

truffle oil (optional)

In medium saucepan, add chicken stock, water, and wine. Bring to boil, cover with lid, and keep on low heat.

Heat olive oil in a medium pot. Add garlic, green onions, leeks, and mushrooms. Cook for 10–12 minutes on medium heat. Cook until onions are translucent, mushrooms are soft, and liquid has dissipated. Add rice and mix all ingredients until rice is coated. Cook until rice is slightly toasted, about 6–8 minutes. Add 1 ladle of hot chicken stock in increments, continually stirring. When risotto has absorbed the liquid, add another ladle of hot stock, continually adding liquid in increments. Repeat this until risotto is almost al dente – (rice is tender to the bite).

To finish risotto, add Parmesan cheese and butter. Mix together for 1 minute. Turn off heat. Serve in bowls.

Optional: Garnish with 2 teaspoons truffle oil drizzled over top of risotto.

SCORE TIP:

MUSHROOM-LEEK RISOTTO

RICE: There are different types of rice that are used for making risotto: Arborio and Carnaroli are two of the most popular varieties. To make a good risotto, you must have rice that is high in starch. These rice varieties are known for their high-starch content. As you add your stock in stages to the rice, the starch is slowly released from the rice and creates that creamy, rich texture that we associate with a risotto dish.

STOCK: There are also many types of stock you can use when making risottos. In this particular dish, I use chicken stock. You can use other types of stock in this recipe: beef stock, lamb stock, or vegetable stock. Beef and lamb stock will give you a more intense flavor and your vegetable stock will be a little milder in taste. Great for vegetarians or vegans. In any risotto recipe, make sure you keep your stock hot.

Ray and...

Whole Wheat Penne with Spicy Puttanesca Sauce and Mussels

Citrus-Herb Salmon

Ray's Famous Chopped Medley Salad

I have to thank my friend, Kenny (aka Baked Stuffed Clams King), for introducing me to this bold, energy-laden, running-machine character. I am truly blessed to have Ray as a friend. I have never met anyone like him in my life. As the saying goes, "Things happen for a reason in life," and I truly believe we were meant to meet and have each other in our lives. If it weren't for Ray, I don't think I would be the runner I am today. Running has become a major part of my life. Ray opened my eyes to a whole new world and pushed me to limits I didn't think possible.

It was early summer, and I had agreed to run a full-fledged marathon with my two crazy Kansas City friends. Now mind you, the agreement was made after I'd had one too many drinks and the superhuman Jenn came into play and took over my brainwaves. I wasn't a runner by any means, and I needed to find a training partner/running buddy to help prepare me for this monstrosity of a race. The major motivator was that we were running in Honolulu and after the marathon we would be lounging by the ocean drinking piña coladas and playing with dolphins. At the time, my longest run had only been four miles and I had no idea how I would pull off the 26.2 miles. I asked Kenny if he knew anyone who was crazier than I was and who would help me train.

Kenny said, "I have the perfect guy for you: Iron Man Ray."

I asked, "Why do you call him Iron Man?"

Kenny said, "He's a machine. He can be out all night partying and drinking and still get up the next morning and run twenty miles. He's definitely going to kick your ass."

I said to Kenny, "Excellent. This is exactly the person I need to motivate and push me. Bring on the Iron Man."

It was about seven on a warm and humid Saturday morning. The sun was just cresting the rolling hills and lush trees in Connecticut. I was on my way to meet the Iron Man. As I pulled into a quiet, barren, office parking lot, a little black Mazda Miata convertible pulled in at the same time. When the Iron Man got out of his car, I expected someone around my age. Ray was a strapping fifty-nine-year-old with the body of Jack Lalanne, a perpetual tan, and surfer blonde hair. Not a bad looking guy.

What was I getting myself into? He looked like a crazy Iron Man and he was about to kick my ass. Why had I signed up to run 26.2 miles? All the negative chatter in my brain was not helping matters and I knew there was no turning back at this point.

As we ran over the next several months leading up to the marathon, I never thought in a million years I would be able to run that many miles at one time. By this point, our training runs were up to fourteen miles, and Ray thought it would be a great idea to run a half-marathon. What? I wasn't ready for a half-marathon. Was he kidding? No, he actually wasn't.

He took the initiative and signed us both up for the race. There was no way out. I had to run. My nerves shot up sky high as if I were being blown out of a cannon.

Race morning came and I met Ray in the small, sleepy Connecticut town where the race was to begin. It was a damp, breezy, chilly morning, and in all honesty I was scared to death to run my first half-marathon race. The sky was overcast and looked as if it would rain any minute. As we made our way to the starting line, many more advanced runners lined up with us. The whole scene was surreal to me. The other runners were doing quick warm up sprints, stretching in all sorts of positions, slurping down endurance gels, and talking smack about their past personal records (PRs). I had knots in my stomach as we toed the starting line. I didn't want to be in the front, for those spots were reserved for the truly fast, Kenyan-like runners. I didn't have a choice of starting spot. The corral letter on our bibs, marked with a huge capital H, indicated that we were in the very last corral, which was reserved for the molasses-slow, old-aged, overweight runners. I felt as if I were at a friend's wedding and placed at the table way in the back with all the crazy relatives nobody liked. While the National Anthem was being played on a cheap boom box with a microphone held to the speaker, the crackly, static sounds of "and the home of the brave" faded in the distance. We were ready to run. The gun went off and so did our Garmin watches. We started our pace very slow, for we had to endure 13.1 miles of hilly terrain. The first five miles were smooth sailing. We had a great pace going, but I was leery of the ominous dark clouds approaching fast.

I said to Ray in between breaths, "Maybe we can try to beat the rain.?

Ray, breathing heavily, replied, "I don't know if we'll make it. We might get a little wet before the finish line."

What? No way. I hadn't signed up for these shenanigans. At mile eight we were still at a steady pace of 10½ minutes/mile. Anyone reading this who is a truly elite, fast runner is probably thinking, my god what a slow-ass pace. But I was proud of what I was doing.

Not one minute after we passed the eight-mile marker, I felt a few drops of rain hit my arm. The sky was completely black at this point and thirty seconds after those few baby drops fell, the sky opened up and the rain poured as if a flood gate had been released. At one point I couldn't even see. The rain was coming down so fast I was blinded by the water pouring into my eyes. Everything on my body was drenched, even down to my underwear. My socks and shoes were soaked and with every step I took, I felt the squishing sensation. Ray was drenched to the bone as well and the miserable look on his face said it all. When we rounded the last corner, I saw the finish line in the distance. I was completely exhausted and was doing a running shuffle at this point. I heard the cheers of the small crowd gathered at the finish line and I started running faster. Ray never left my side during the race and we both crossed at the same time. We finished the race in two hours and twelve minutes. We were soaked, exhausted, cold, and ready to go home. A hot shower, some food, and a shot of whisky sounded good to me.

When I crossed the finished line, I was very proud of myself for running 13.1 miles. It was my first, official, long-distance race. If Ray had not been there, cheering and coaching me until the very end, I would not be where I am today. After the half-marathon, we resumed training and added more miles to our training runs. Almost all through our runs, we talked about food, recipes, and their preparation. This really kept our minds off the pain and the pure exhaustion. I would always tell Ray what new and exciting recipes I had created that particular week or had created in the past. He heard me describe all the recipes and details that are in this book.

Ray changed my life forever. He really believed in me and knew I had the drive, motivation, and endurance to run. There were so many times I wanted to quit and give up, but he didn't let me. He always cheered me up and told me that I could do it. After the marathon, and still to this day, we run together. He is a running machine. Thanks, Ray. I couldn't have done it without you.

whole wheat penne with spicy puttanesca sauce and mussels

WHOLE WHEAT PENNE WITH
SPICY PUTTANESCA SAUCE AND MUSSELS
YIELD: 4 SERVINGS

1 lb. of whole wheat penne

PUTTANESCA SAUCE

2 tablespoons olive oil

1 teaspoon garlic, chopped

½ red onion, chopped

2 tablespoons capers

½ cup black olives, chopped

1 lemon, juiced

½ teaspoon lemon zest

2 (15 oz.) cans stewed tomatoes

1 small tomato, diced

¼ cup red wine

1 teaspoon balsamic vinegar

1 can artichoke hearts, drained and chopped

1 lb. fresh mussels

salt and pepper

Heat olive oil in large sauté pan on high. Add garlic and onions and cook for 2 minutes. Reduce heat to medium-high. Add capers, olives, lemon juice, and lemon zest. Mix together and cook for a few minutes. Add the remainder of the ingredients, except mussels; stir and simmer for 25 minutes. Season with salt and pepper to taste.

Bring a pot of water to boil and cook pasta according to package instructions while sauce simmers. Drain pasta and reserve.

Turn heat up slightly on sauce and add mussels. Cover with lid and let steam until opened, about 3–4 minutes. Serve over pasta.

SCORE TIP:

Puttanesca sauce was originally created in Naples in the late 1940s–early 50s. I have read several stories about how this sauce was actually created and all of them seem to fit together, just like the ingredients in this recipe. The word "puttanesca" translates as "whore." In the brothels in Naples, the prostitutes would make this sauce to lure and entice potential clients. The prostitutes also made the sauce for themselves because it was quick, easy, and kept the interruption of their business to a minimum. The basic ingredients in a true puttanesca sauce are tomatoes, capers, anchovies, olives, basil, and oregano. In this recipe, I have omitted the anchovies, but if you love these little critters, feel free to add them in. One whole anchovy, finely chopped, will suffice, or you can use 1 teaspoon of anchovy paste.

CITRUS-HERB SALMON

YIELD: 4 SERVINGS

4 (5–6 oz.) salmon fillets, with skins

2 tablespoons olive oil

1½ teaspoons salt

¼ teaspoon ground pepper

1 lemon, squeezed

1 orange, squeezed

½ lime, squeezed

1 tablespoon balsamic vinegar

¼ cup pomegranate juice

¼ cup fresh basil leaves, chopped

¼ cup fresh parsley, chopped

2 tablespoons fresh chives, chopped

2 tablespoons green onions, chopped

⅓ cup olive oil

1 tablespoon grain mustard

1 teaspoon hot sauce

salt and pepper

In baking dish, take salmon fillets and coat with 2 tablespoons of olive oil. Sprinkle fillets with salt and pepper. Squeeze lemon, orange, lime, balsamic vinegar, and pomegranate juices into small bowl. Mix together and pour mixture over the top of each fillet. Put in fridge for 30 minutes to marinate. In small bowl, add all herbs, green onions, olive oil, mustard, and hot sauce. Add salt and pepper to taste. Blend until incorporated. Take salmon fillets out of fridge and spread herb mixture over the top of each fillets. Bake at 375 degrees for 7–10 minutes or until desired consistency. Let rest for 1 minute before serving.

CITRUS-HERB SALMON

If you want to take your salmon to a whole new level, try cooking it on a cedar plank. These are found everywhere now. Try your local kitchen store or your local hardware store. Remember to get an untreated cedar plank. You need a big enough piece for 3–4 medium-sized salmon fillets. First, soak your plank in water for 20–30 minutes. Make sure your salmon is well coated with oil before going onto the plank. The plank can go into the oven or onto your grill. Cedar planks are not just for salmon. Try cooking chicken, steaks, pork, or even tofu on these planks.

RAY'S FAMOUS CHOPPED MEDLEY SALAD

YIELD: 4 SERVINGS

1 cup chopped carrots

⅓ cup red onions, diced small

½ cup cucumbers, diced small

½ cup cherry tomatoes, halved

1½ cups grilled eggplant, chopped

1 cup grilled zucchini, chopped

½ cup green pepper, diced small

⅓ cup kalamata olives, pits removed, chopped

½ cup feta cheese, crumbled

⅓ cup torn basil leaves

½ cup extra-virgin olive oil

⅓ cup balsamic vinegar

salt and freshly ground black pepper to taste

In large bowl, add all ingredients except for olive oil and balsamic. Mix together until all ingredients are incorporated.

In small bowl, add balsamic, salt, and pepper. Whisk in olive oil slowly. Toss the vegetables with the dressing. Serve.

SCORE TIP:

RAY'S FAMOUS CHOPPED MEDLEY SALAD

Ray's running training tip 1: when enduring any distance running, whether it's a training run, fun run, or a race, Ray's training tip will help you get ahead and beat your competitors. Drink a few glasses of wine the night before. The sugars in the wine will help fuel your body and help you conquer those tough hills and long distances. Drink white wine for shorter distances and red wine for longer distances. I can personally say from experience that champagne really helped me achieve a PR. I had a few glasses of champagne the night prior to the race. I don't know if it was just a good day for my body, but I ran my little heart out during the New York City half-marathon.

Disclaimer: this theory was only tested among a few individuals. We do not encourage drinking before a race. We encourage safe training practices.

Big Burt and...

Fresh-off-the-Boat, Seared Coriander-Cilantro Ahi Tuna with Citrus-Wasabi Glaze

My girlfriend, Trish, and I met one Friday afternoon for some TGIF cocktails at our local "regal beagle" tavern in Connecticut. After a few hours of blowing off steam (which we needed to do) with our favorite cocktails in hand, one of the tavern regulars Trish had become semi-friendly with came over to say hello. Big Burt was a character. He was a 6-foot-4, dark-haired fellow who looked like a forty-something virgin. He was dressed like a lumberjack and thought he was God's gift to women. After being introduced to him, I was convinced he was just a little off center and not all there upstairs.

Big Burt was an avid fisherman and started talking about his adventures on the open sea. When he mentioned deep sea fishing, it sparked some interest because it was on my bucket list. After a few hours during which Big Burt talked our ears off about his fishing excursions and four cocktails later, Trish and I planned to go deep sea fishing off the coast of Cape Cod. I called Kenny and Trish called her boyfriend to see if they were interested in participating in this insane adventure. We had five people for the trip, and we were ready to start planning.

Burt mentioned that he had a friend who was the captain of a boat in Scituate, Massachusetts. His name was Captain Jack of Half Fast Charters. Trish found a great rental house right on the ocean in Scituate. We had two months to get ourselves psyched for the trip. I was finally going deep sea fishing and I couldn't bear the wait. I was going to be able to check this off my list.

The day approached and we piled in Kenny's SUV to head up to Scituate. Burt was already up at the rental house and called to tell us how awesome it was. He told us to look for his "big-ass green van" in front of the house. It was around 10:00 p.m. when we rolled into the sleepy, picturesque town of Scituate, which looked like your typical New England harbor town but had unique seaside charm. I felt as if I were on the movie set of *The Truman Show*. As Kenny followed his MapQuest directions because he didn't believe in GPS devices, we turned down the street our rental house was on. It was so dark that it was hard to make out the addresses on the houses, but I said to Kenny, "Big Burt said to look for the big-ass green van parked in the drive-way."

Lo and behold, we spotted the big-ass green van. What a beauty it was. It looked like the green machine van from *Scooby Doo*. It definitely fit the mold for Big Burt. We had finally arrived. We were steps away from the ocean and the sound of the waves crashing onto the shore put me in relaxation mode. The house was literally ten feet from the water and I thought I might never want to go back to my other life. Maybe I would just quit my job and become a fisherman.

The night before the fishing extravaganza, we decided to stay in and cook. I made everyone my famous mojitos. We had to cut ourselves off at 9:00 p.m. because we didn't want to feel sick on the boat. To go along with the theme of the deep sea fishing weekend, I decided to come up with a fresh tuna recipe and complementary sauce. I knew the tuna steaks we had purchased at the local fish market would be "fresh off the boat." I marinated the tuna steaks in fresh and dried herbs and squeezed a little lemon to bring out the taste of the tuna. To complement the tuna, I made up a citrus-wasabi sauce that would take it to the next level. Dinner was a hit among the group. With all our bellies full, we polished off the last of the mojitos. Before we went to bed that night, Burt asked us all if we would refrain from bringing any bananas onto the boat. Puzzled and just plain boggled by this request, I asked him why. He said superstitious fisherman believe a banana is a bad omen and brings extremely bad luck. After Trish and I did a thorough investigation of our beach bungalow, and I contemplated the sanity of Big Burt, we determined the premises were clear of all banana products. So what could possibly go wrong on the boat?

Morning approached very fast and Kenny was up at 3:30 a.m. making coffee for everyone. After we gathered our stuff and packed the car, we were on our way to the boat. Captain Jack awaited us and gave us all a very warm welcome. He introduced us to his first mate, who looked like a homeless mob boss who had just killed someone and was three sheets to the wind. Captain Jack led us down a dark cement path to the dock area. For a late September morning, it was very cold, and my idea of wearing my bikini that day, thinking I just might get a few hours to lie out on the boat, was pretty much a figment of my imagination at this point.

Captain Jack said to all of us, as he stood in front of a boat that looked as if it had been hit by a tornado, "Here is Ms. Bessie. She might look old and decrepit, but she will take care of you out there on the sea."

Wow! Ms. Bessie looked as if she were about two hundred years old and was very small compared to the other massive, brand-new, shiny fishing boats that were docked. I looked at Trish and said, "Do you think this boat is safe? I hope we don't sink."

Captain Jack finished up his safety check on Ms. Bessie and yelled at the top of his lungs, "Full steam ahead! Ahoy, maties."

The engine roared like a massive semi truck and I wondered how something so old could sound like that. We made our way out of the harbor and into the black, open sea.

The sun was rising slowly in the distance and the peace of the ocean made me feel very calm. I had taken my prescription-strength Dramamine and I felt invincible. A few hours in, the sun was rising, but the fish were not biting. Captain Jack drove the boat farther out, and by this time we were thirty miles offshore. The waves crested at eight to ten feet, and we were all tossed around like rag dolls.

Starting to feel a little queasy, I headed toward the small cabin to take another Dramamine. I made Trish's boyfriend grab my bag from underneath the deck because I couldn't bear going inside the cabin. As I turned around after Trish's boyfriend gave me the bag, I saw the homeless-mob-boss-looking mate chomping on a fresh banana. As I stood there stunned and frozen, Trish's boyfriend caught me gazing at the first mate and he stood motionless as well. We couldn't believe our eyes. We were all doomed, and all hell was about to break loose. Like clockwork, without warning, all four of us were hanging over the side of the boat in ten-foot waves, throwing up and hanging on for dear life. I was holding onto Kenny's sweatshirt so tightly that I choked him as I threw up. The curse was true. While we were all throwing up over the side of the boat, Big Burt, who was wearing BluBlocker sunglasses and eating a massive sandwich and drinking a beer, had a shit-eating grin on his face.

After we threw up for the eighth time, we told the captain to turn the boat around and head into shore. Mind you, we had caught absolutely no fish and we had a three-hour trip back to the shore. My dreams were shattered. I wasn't going to catch my 400-pound tuna and be the hero of the trip. As we traveled back to shore, I didn't take my eyes off the horizon, and all the while, my dream floated away. Finally, I could see the shore.

I shouted, "Land! Land!"

Everyone let out a sigh of relief. Captain Jack gingerly docked the boat. I was so thankful to place my feet on stable ground that I lay on the cold dock. I didn't move for a good five minutes and was very thankful that my queasiness was subsiding. What a ride we'd had.

I looked at Trish and said, "Okay, we can check that off our bucket list." Check.

FRESH-OFF-THE-BOAT, SEARED CORIANDER-CILANTRO AHI TUNA WITH CITRUS-WASABI GLAZE

YIELD: 4 SERVINGS

4 (4–6 oz.) Ahi tuna steaks, fresh off the boat

2 teaspoons ground coriander

2 tablespoons fresh cilantro,

chopped

1 tablespoon fresh chives, chopped

1 teaspoon black pepper

1 ½ teaspoons salt

1 teaspoon cumin

½ teaspoon red pepper flakes

1 lemon, squeezed

In a small bowl, combine all spices and mix well. Coat tuna evenly with spice mixture on both sides. Set aside in fridge for 30 minutes. Heat grill to 375 degrees, squeeze lemon juice on each tuna steak, and grill tuna steaks until desired consistency. Pour citrus-wasabi glaze over the top.

SCORE TIP:

FRESH-OFF-THE-BOAT, SEARED CORIANDER-CILANTRO AHI TUNA

When purchasing fresh tuna, remember these tips:

1. Make sure the tuna smells fresh like the ocean and does not have a fishy smell. A fishy smell means your tuna is old and is going bad.

2. Make sure the color of the tuna is bright, shiny, and pink.

3. Always buy your tuna from a reputable seafood market. Don't be afraid to ask your fishmonger where your tuna came from or when he received it.

4. When you get home from the market, make sure you put your tuna on ice, in the fridge, if it's going to be several hours before you prepare it.

CITRUS-WASABI GLAZE

1 cup orange juice

½ cup grapefruit juice

1 tablespoon lemon juice

2 tablespoons honey

1 tablespoon apple cider vinegar

½ tablespoon wasabi paste

salt and pepper

In saucepan, add all ingredients, mix well, and bring to a boil. Reduce heat to medium-low and simmer until liquid is reduced to ½ cup. Serve hot over tuna.

SCORE TIP:

CITRUS-WASABI GLAZE

Wasabi powder is available at most local markets. Wasabi is a variety of green horseradish only grown in Japan. Many wasabi powders and paste products that are available in your local markets contain very little or no real wasabi and are made of colored horseradish. Wasabi powder has to be mixed with water to gain that pungent, hot flavor. When adding water to the powder, you want to create a paste-like texture. Authentic wasabi is a root and is extremely expensive and rare to find in the United States. So, when you go to your local sushi joint, don't be scared to ask your server if they have the real deal. I was in a local place in Chicago and I asked our server if they had fresh, shaved wasabi and lo and behold, fresh wasabi was on my table. What a treat it was with my sushi. It takes it to a whole new level. Delicious!

Kenny and...

Black Bean, Corn, and Roasted Red Pepper Salad, Topped with Lime-Tequila Grilled Shrimp

Matambritos de Chancho and Pico de Gallo (Argentine Flank Steak with Chimichurri)

Grilled Fruit over Angel Food Cake with Sangria Sauce

Kenny's Famous Sangria

These dishes were inspired by my cooking show pilot, *First Bites*. I spent months and months planning this show on my own and decided to research my past life before I entered the culinary world. Tom, who owned a film-production company in Kansas City, was my best prospect for the job. I asked him if he would like to come up to Connecticut with all of his film equipment and shoot the pilot. After some negotiating, Tom and his cousin made arrangements to do it. This was my dream and passion, and I was determined to make the pilot happen.

During the months when I planned my pilot, I was still dating Brad. I thought a great location for the show would be in his parents' kitchen. The mansion was the perfect setting and would set the mood for the first scene. As we pulled into the mini-White House, we were greeted by Brad's parents. They were very kind and helped us carry all the equipment and food in. We were on a schedule and had five hours to get two scenes done. The dishes that I made on camera were penne with a puttanesca sauce and mussels, and panzanella salad.

After we filmed the final closing segment, Tom yelled, "Cut and that's a wrap!" Two down and two more segments to go. Then it was party time. We diligently packed the car, said our goodbyes to Brad's parents, and headed to our final location, Kenny's house. We were going to shoot our last few segments there and have a huge party afterward to celebrate. At this point, I was ready for a cocktail because Brad and I were on the verge of breaking up. We had fought the whole day on the phone.

The filming went flawlessly at Kenny's house and the baked clam expert greeted all the guests who had arrived for the party. In the last segment of the show, Kenny and I were going to make his famous sangria. His libation recipe was legendary, just like his recipe for baked stuffed clams. We had a captive audience by the time we shot this segment. No one was feeling any pain because of the very strong margaritas and sangria that Kenny had made.

Kenny's sangria recipe inspired my sangria sauce for the grilled fruit dessert. It's an amazing dish with many memories surrounding it.

black bean, corn, and roasted red pepper salad, topped with lime-tequila grilled shrimp

BLACK BEAN, CORN, AND ROASTED RED PEPPER SALAD, TOPPED WITH LIME-TEQUILA GRILLED SHRIMP

YIELD: 4 SERVINGS

1 (15 oz.) can black beans, drained

1 (15 oz.) can corn, drained

1 large green pepper, medium diced

½ medium red onion, diced small

½ cup roasted red peppers, chopped

½ teaspoon garlic, chopped

1 tablespoon jalapeño, seeds and white pith removed, chopped

¼ cup olive oil

2 tablespoons balsamic vinegar

1 teaspoon hot sauce

1 lime, squeezed

salt and pepper

SHRIMP

12 large raw shrimp, peeled, deveined

2 large limes, squeezed

⅓ cup of tequila

salt and pepper

Preheat grill to 375 degrees.

To make shrimp: in medium bowl, place shrimp, lime juice, tequila, salt, and pepper. Incorporate all ingredients. Let marinate for 20 minutes in fridge.

To make salad: in medium bowl, mix all ingredients well. Put in fridge for one hour.

Take shrimp and grill for 3–5 minutes per side until firm, pink, and thoroughly cooked. Don't have a grill? Just sauté in medium-sized sauté pan on medium-high heat for 3–5 minutes per side until thoroughly cooked. Remove shrimp and cool. Put salad into bowls and top with shrimp.

BLACK BEAN, CORN, AND ROASTED RED PEPPER SALAD, TOPPED WITH LIME-TEQUILA GRILLED SHRIMP

When the shrimp have marinated, they will change to a pale white. The citric acid in the lime causes the shrimp to become denatured and they pickle or "cook" without heat. This is what the dish ceviche is based on. The lime juice alters the structure of the shrimp, making it more opaque and firm, as if it had been cooked with heat. Whether you are making this recipe or you are making ceviche, it's important to start with the freshest seafood. Always buy your seafood from a reputable fish market. In this recipe, even though the lime juice starts the "cooking" process, I grill the shrimp to give it more flavor and depth.

matambritos de chancho and pico de gallo (argentine flank steak with chimichurri)

MATAMBRITOS DE CHANCHO AND PICO DE GALLO (ARGENTINE FLANK STEAK WITH CHIMICHURRI)

YIELD: 4–6 SERVINGS

BRINE

3 lb. flank steak

¾ gallon water

½ cup sugar

⅓ cup salt

1 teaspoon garlic salt

1 tablespoon whole pepper corns

2 tablespoons Worcestershire sauce

1 tablespoon hot sauce

¼ cup apple cider vinegar

CHIMICHURRI

2 tablespoons olive oil

1 tablespoon garlic, chopped

1½ cups yellow onion, diced small

½ cup fresh parsley, chopped

⅓ cup fresh cilantro, chopped

1 tablespoon fresh mint, chopped

1 teaspoon lemon zest

1 tablespoon lemon juice

1 tablespoon apple cider vinegar

⅓ cup olive oil

1 tablespoon chopped jalapeños

½ teaspoon each paprika, dried oregano, dried basil.

¼ teaspoon cayenne pepper

¼ teaspoon black pepper

salt

To make brine: fill large container with water. Add sugar and salt to water and stir until dissolved. Add the rest of the brine ingredients and mix together with salt/sugar solution. Put meat into solution, cover, and put into fridge for 24–48 hours. (The longer you leave the meat in the brine mixture, the more intense the flavor of the meat.)

To make chimichurri topping: heat 2 tablespoons olive oil in large sauté pan on medium-high. Add garlic and onions. Lower heat to medium and sauté for 15 minutes. Take off heat and cool. Mix remainder of ingredients in medium bowl. When garlic and onion mixture cools, add to herb mixture. Stir together until incorporated. Put in fridge.

When meat has thoroughly marinated, take out of brine solution, and pat dry with paper towel. Discard brine solution. Heat grill to 375 degrees. Cook meat to medium-rare/medium.

Take off grill and let rest for five minutes before slicing. Cut against the grain into ¼-inch thick strips.

Put slices onto plate and top meat with chimichurri mix. Serve with flour tortillas, sour cream, and tomatoes.

PICO DE GALLO

6 vine-ripened tomatoes, diced small

½ medium white onion, diced small

1 small jalapeño, white pith and

seeds removed, diced small

1 teaspoon garlic, chopped

2 tablespoons chopped cilantro

¼ cup white vinegar

½ lime, squeezed

½ teaspoon red pepper flakes

salt and pepper

In medium-sized bowl, mix all ingredients well until incorporated and refrigerate for one hour before serving.

Serve with tortilla chips.

SCORE TIP:

MATAMBRITOS DE CHANCHO AND PICO DE GALLO (ARGENTINE FLANK STEAK WITH CHIMICHURRI)

Chimichurri is a thick, spicy, herb sauce used traditionally in Argentina as a marinade, condiment, and grilling sauce for meats. It can also be used as a dipping sauce. Chimichurri is the most popular meat topping in Argentina. It can be found on pretty much every restaurant table. Usually it's served on beef, but it is also served on chicken, pork, veal, and eggs. The basic components of a chimichurri are parsley, olive oil, garlic, vinegar, herbs, and onions.

Chimichurri is like our American barbeque sauce. Every region and all individual cooks have their own variation. Some are better than others.

If the brine part of the recipe is too time consuming, do the following: in a small bowl add Worcestershire sauce, hot sauce, vinegar, pepper corns, cloves, and ¼ cup olive oil. Use the same measurements given in the recipe. Mix ingredients together and brush both sides of meat. Salt and pepper to taste. Let sit for an hour.

Brining the meat really helps tenderize it and adds a lot of flavor. So if you have time, I highly suggest taking this easy step.

grilled fruit over angel food cake with sangria sauce

GRILLED FRUIT OVER ANGEL FOOD CAKE WITH SANGRIA SAUCE

YIELD: 6 SERVINGS

1 pineapple, top and bottom removed, skin removed, cut lengthwise into strips, ½-inch wide

2 peaches, halved and pitted

1 mango, peeled, cut lengthwise, ½-inch wide

⅓ cup olive oil

1 lemon

1 cup red seedless grapes, halved

½ cup chopped kiwi

½ cup blueberries

1 angel food cake, whole

SANGRIA SAUCE

½ cup sugar

1 cup water

⅓ cup peach schnapps

½ cup champagne or white wine

½ cup cranberry juice

1 cup grape juice

1 lime, squeezed

Preheat grill to 375 degrees.

In small bowl, add olive oil and squeeze lemon into oil. Mix together until incorporated. Brush mango, pineapple, and peaches with lemon oil and set aside.

To make sangria sauce: heat water and sugar in a medium saucepan on medium-high. Dissolve sugar and add the rest of the ingredients. Bring to a boil and then reduce heat to a medium simmer until sauce reduces to 1 cup. Cool completely; sauce will thicken as it cools.

Grill or sauté fruit until light golden brown on all sides. Let cool. Cut up in bite-sized pieces and put in bowl along with rest of fruit. Mix together.

Cut angel food cake into individual pieces. Sprinkle fruit mixture over each piece of angel food cake and drizzle sangria sauce over top.

SCORE TIP:

GRILLED FRUIT OVER ANGEL FOOD CAKE WITH SANGRIA SAUCE

I would not suggest using canned fruit in this recipe. Canned fruit is loaded with sugary syrup and the fruit tastes very soft and mushy. You want to use the freshest fruit possible. If you can't find the fruit in your local markets or it's out of season and you don't want to pay an arm and leg for it, here are some other suggestions for replacements:

PEACHES: replace with plums or nectarines

KIWI: replace with oranges

MANGO: replace with bananas

BLUEBERRIES: replace with Craisins

KENNY'S FAMOUS SANGRIA

YIELD: 4–6 SERVINGS

1 bottle of red wine
(preferably a light pinot noir)

⅓ cup peach schnapps

¼ cup triple sec

1 orange, sliced

1 lime, sliced

½ cup orange juice

½ cup cranberry juice

1 tablespoon agave nectar

1 cup grape soda

Ice

In large pitcher, add red wine, schnapps, triple sec, and cut up fruit. Stir together. Add rest of ingredients except grape soda.

Let rest in fridge for a few hours. Add grape soda and ice, stir together and serve immediately.

Chapter 4

Grilled Pizzas with an Assortment of Toppings

Maple-Cured Salmon with Maple Glaze

Wild Mushroom Risotto

Lobster Spring Rolls with Mango-Pineapple Chutney

Wild Mushroom Salad with Mesclun-Frisée Mix, Lemon Vinaigrette, and Blue Cheese Balls

Chunky Fruit Soup Infused with Ginger-Lemon Syrup

Stoker Spinach Salad with Warm Bacon Dressing, Caramelized Red Onion Bits, and a Fried Egg

Pulled Pork with Bourbon Barbeque Sauce

Cranberry-Vanilla Dressing over Mesclun Greens with Herb, Hazelnut, Goat Cheese Truffles

Pork Tenderloin Stuffed with Bacon, Spinach, and Feta Cheese

Sweet Potato and Sausage Gratin with Savory Maple Glaze

Toasted Crostini Topped with Prosciutto and Honey, with Goat Cheese-Mascarpone Whip

Fruit Salad with Bean Sprouts and Radicchio, Drizzled with Honey

Pesto Fusilli with Potatoes, Green Beans, and Peas, with Shaved Parmesan cheese

These recipes are dedicated to my loving, supportive family, especially my parents. They are the rock in my world and without them I would not be where I am today. Thanks to everyone in my family for making these memories come together.

The family is a haven in a heartless world.　　*—Attributed to Christopher Lasch*

A Family Party and...
Grilled Pizzas with an Assortment of Toppings

My family had never organized a party before, and we were stoked for the first one. The Stoker Extravaganza was gearing up to be the party of the year. We weren't celebrating anything monumental but wanted a reason to gather all of our friends and family to have a memorable Fourth of July weekend. The party planning began a few months prior to my flying into Cleveland. I was fresh out of culinary school and I wanted to showcase what I had learned at the CIA. After coming up with a tentative menu, I suggested to my mother that she hire a polka band for the party. Cleveland may not have as big a Polish population as Chicago, but it still boasts a large number in its own right. There are also many Slovenians, the other side of my heritage. So we thought, what better way to celebrate the birth of America and where my family originated than a huge party?

My mom got to work and asked for suggestions from her Polish and Slovenian friends. The recommendation was unanimous: The Corky Gordic Polka Band. We were told they were fairly inexpensive and would rock the house. I couldn't really see a polka band "rocking the house," but my mom's friends insisted they could even make Queen Elizabeth get up and dance. If you've never heard polka music, think of lively accordions, energetic pianos, and people clapping while others dance. It's almost impossible not to enjoy.

We booked the band, and I started focusing on the most important thing for the party: the food. I decided to make some easy dishes, but wanted to put a few twists on the typical party food. I made a variety of appetizers including my famous hummus, tomatillo-avocado, yellow tomato ginger-chipotle salsa and guajillo salsa, gourmet chicken wings, Funyun and pork rind chicken bites, cucumber cups, crudités with a chipotle-bacon dip and my undiscovered grilled pizzas. I hadn't yet experimented with the grilled pizzas. I learned this technique at school and it was going to be the first time I had tested the recipe out on my own.

My two aunts came over a few hours before the party and started to help me get everything ready. Aunt Gail, who is a fabulous self-taught cook, helped me out tremendously in the kitchen. She has the knack and skill of a true professional chef. Aunt Carolyn, who makes a couple of other appearances in this book, has been hailed as our family's honorary "firefighter." She got the nickname because she tends to leave her kitchen when she's cooking and comes back to a small fire she needs to put out.

While the aunts worked away like newly hired prep chefs in a restaurant kitchen, my mom was outside helping the polka band get set up. My parents had a very large, open stone patio and since the weather had actually cooperated for once, we were setting up outside. My mom claims the "good weather" came because she put her rosary in our tree. According to an old Catholic Slovenian custom, putting a rosary in a tree on your property will bring good weather. For the party, I wanted to have a few "adult beverage" stations. One station for beer and wine, one for mojitos, and the other for my dad's friend, Paulie. Paulie, aka Paulie "Walnuts," made a prize-winning grappa in his basement. He had won many awards for his homemade grappa in the state of Ohio and he was looking to self-promote that golden prize—a golden prize that tasted like fuel siphoned right out of the tank of a 747 jet and could make hair grow on the chest of anyone regardless of their gender, but a golden prize nonetheless.

It was approaching 6:30 p.m. and the party was starting. The polka band was warming up and since their circus-like banjo music would be filling the entire neighborhood all night, my mom decided to invite all the neighbors so the police wouldn't get called. The two line cooks, aka the aunts, had finished their last tasks and we were ready to start shuttling everything outside. Like an executive chef in a high volume kitchen, I barked orders left and right. I yelled urgently for Aunt Carolyn and my mother to take everything outside except for the grilled pizza ingredients—it was going to be my grand finale, after all. I was a little apprehensive about making the grilled pizzas because it was my first time and it was a large function. If these people didn't like the food, I was definitely going to hear about it. What was I thinking?

The party was in full swing by 8:00 p.m. and the guests were taking everything in: the good food, libations, and the unforgettable sounds of the Corky Gordic Polka music. I saw smiles and dreamy looks on older family members' faces, and I knew the band brought them back to their younger days. Paulie's prize-winning grappa was a big hit with everyone and I could tell it had affected a handful of people. As I brought out more food to refresh what was missing, I saw a few of my older relatives who had participated in the grappa festivities forming their own dance floor. They were true polka aficionados, mind you, and they knew what they were doing. As four of them broke out with their best moves, six of my other relatives formed a circle around them. They were clapping, stomping their feet, and yelling out in Polish.

I made my way through the crowd to light the grill as it was nearly time to prepare the pizzas. As I turned to go inside to get the ingredients, I saw my father trying to dance in the middle of the polka circle with one of my older aunts. The band was playing a fast song, and to my amazement, they both were keeping up with the beat. I'm sure the grappa had something to do with my father's newly found rhythm. My mom, who hadn't touched the grappa, just shook her head and went inside to help me.

When I got back into the kitchen, lovely Aunt Carolyn was already there getting the pizza ingredients ready. She knew it was showtime and she told everyone at the party to save room because, in her words, "the most unbelievable pizzas you've ever had are coming up."

I said to my aunt, "I'm a little nervous to make these. I've only made them in school, so I'm not sure if they're even going to turn out."

"Oh Jennifer, you are a great chef. Of course they will turn out," she said nonchalantly as she carried the stacked dough and olive oil out the patio door. With new-found delusional confidence, I told myself she was right.

As we all marched outside, ingredients in hand, one of my mom's friends shouted at the top of her lungs, "Oh my, it's the legendary pizzas!"

What? "Legendary pizzas?" I couldn't begin to imagine what kind of story my aunts and mother had told these people. So much for confidence.

We made our way to the grill area and since the grilled pizzas required a lot of moving parts, we set up our station around the grill. The pizza dough was rolled out in oddly shaped circles, stacked on top of each other. Toppings were in separate bowls, and the extra olive oil, towels, cutting boards, and knives were all together on one big metal tray.

Because of how I rolled out the dough, it took the three of us to get it onto the grill. We each took a corner of the oily, stretched out dough and lay it gingerly on the grill. I could taste success. The first step was over, and I thought it had gone quite smoothly. As we were ready to flip the monstrosity over, we each picked up a spatula. We lifted the grill lid and the three of us flipped the dough over. After the dough was flipped, we added toppings, and closed the lid to finish the cooking. At this point, the drunken polka partygoers were all gathered around the grill as if they were watching someone's phone displaying the latest and greatest YouTube video.

Next came the hard part: removing the entire pie safely and trying to maintain the presentation. Aunt Carolyn was ready with the cutting board and Aunt Gail and I were armed with spatulas. I realized this would have been a hell of a lot easier with perfectly round, smaller rolled out dough, but I had rolled out massive, oddly shaped semicircular pieces and it was becoming a challenge.

I told the aunts, "In a one-two-three motion, Aunt Gail and I will lift with spatulas and slide onto the cutting board, while Aunt Carolyn holds the cutting board to catch the pizza."

With the crowd looking on suspiciously, I said, "Okay, here we go, one…two…three…"

We picked up the pizza on either side and slid it to the cutting board my aunt was holding. As we slid the pizza toward the board, I knew we'd be victorious. It was but a second after I had that thought when Aunt Carolyn's hand somehow hit the scalding hot pizza sliding off the grill, and the whole cutting board fell. Pizza and all went crashing to the ground. The crowd all groaned in unison. All I could do was pick up the pieces and try it again.

"No worries," I said to my aunts and the crowd. "The first one's always the tester. Here comes the real deal!"

All smiles, we tried it again and by the time the ninth pizza came off the grill, we were professional pizzeria chefs. We were cranking them out so fast you could have sworn we all had past experience at a popular New York pizzeria. The guests either really liked the pizza, or were so drunk they wanted to eat everything in sight.

It was approaching 1:00 a.m. and the party was winding down. The majority of people had left except for a handful of my family and the polka band members.

My mom said to me, "Where is your father? I haven't seen him in a while. We need more help cleaning this place up."

"I have no idea where he is. Maybe he's still outside with the band."

"No, I just looked outside and he's not there. Everyone has left."

She left the kitchen and headed toward the stairs. "I'll be right back," she said in an annoyed voice. She found him upstairs sleeping on of a pile of purses. Apparently he'd had his share of grappa and polka dancing for the evening. My mom had to clean the backyard by herself, but my dad is now forced to wear a T-shirt that reads, "Don't feed me grappa," at every party.

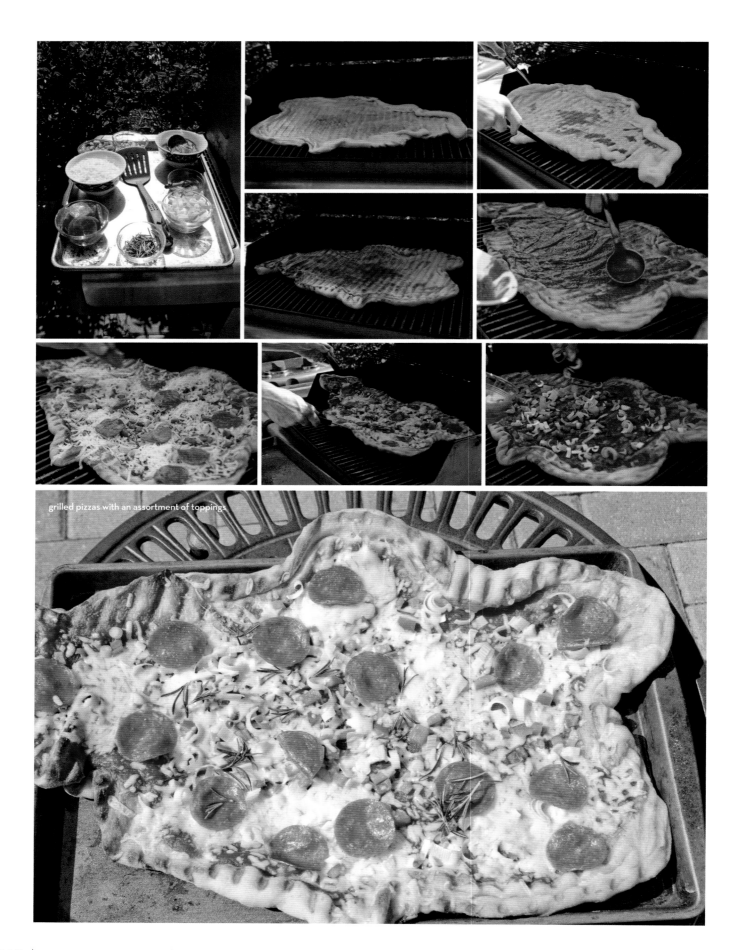

grilled pizzas with an assortment of toppings

GRILLED PIZZAS WITH AN ASSORTMENT OF TOPPINGS

YIELD: 4–6 SERVINGS

2–3 premade pizza doughs, white or wheat (Trader Joe's brand of dough is good or any frozen dough, allow to thaw)

olive oil

flour

toppings of your choice (see list below)

Preheat grill to 350 degrees.

Flour counter and sprinkle flour onto dough. Roll out dough until it forms a circle or square, not too thin, not too thick. Brush both sides with olive oil. Stack on top of each other with plastic wrap in between. Prepare your desired toppings and put into individuals bowls.

GRILLING: Lay your dough on grill and close lid. Grill 3–5 minutes and flip over when dough has browned and is crisp underneath. When you flip over the dough, add toppings of your choice, then close lid for another 3–5 minutes. When pizza is done, remove carefully with a few spatulas and allow to rest for a minute before cutting.

TOPPING CHOICES:

cooked, crisp bacon

cooked sausage

goat cheese

sautéed mushrooms

pepperoni

green onions

red onions

cheddar cheese

mozzarella

fresh tomatoes

barbeque pulled pork

white alfredo sauce

pesto sauce

marinara

grilled vegetables

ham

sun-dried tomatoes

olives

pulled pork

SCORE TIP:

GRILLED PIZZAS WITH AN ASSORTMENT OF TOPPINGS

The best dough to get for your grilled pizzas—and yes here comes the plug—is Trader Joe's. They make the best basic white dough. It comes frozen; it tastes delicious; and it's cheap. What more can you want, right? If you don't have a Trader Joe's in your area, any premade, frozen pizza dough will work, or if you have time, feel free to whip up your own dough. After you have thawed your dough completely, flour both sides, roll out with a rolling pin, and make sure you brush olive oil on both sides before grilling or you will have a burned, nasty mess on your grill. I suggest using white dough rather than wheat when grilling.

If you don't have a rolling pin on hand, try using a wine bottle or a bottle of some sort. If you don't care about the label on your wine bottle, or you're going to drink wine with your pizza, this will show your guests all the hard work that you put into making your pizza. Just be careful when using a wine bottle not to press to hard.

original recipe photos

CHRISTMAS AND...

MAPLE-CURED SALMON WITH MAPLE GLAZE

WILD MUSHROOM RISOTTO

LOBSTER SPRING ROLLS WITH MANGO-PINEAPPLE CHUTNEY

WILD MUSHROOM SALAD WITH MESCLUN-FRISÉE MIX, LEMON VINAIGRETTE, AND BLUE CHEESE BALLS

CHUNKY FRUIT SOUP INFUSED WITH GINGER-LEMON SYRUP

As in most families who celebrate it, Christmas in my family is highly revered. My mother outdoes herself nearly every year. She decorates the house inside and out. I imagine she gets a second wind, judging from the empty bottles of eggnog I've found on more than one occasion. The lights gleam, gifts are neatly wrapped, and the house smells of delicious spices. Most important, it's a time when my whole family can get together. There's nothing better. This particular year, I was recruited to prepare a four-course dinner for my parents, aunts, uncles, cousins, and some of my parents' closest friends. I really wanted to bring everyone together for the holidays, make them something very special, and create memories that would last a lifetime.

I needed all the help I could get, so my father was delighted when I asked him to pair champagne and wine with each course. While he's an ER doctor by vocation, he's also the guy who drives a pickup truck and wears denim overalls. About ten years ago, he became interested in wine. He's been lucky enough to travel all over the world trying wines in numerous different countries. He has a photographic memory, so he's retained everything he's learned about it. He's able to talk about different flavors and origins with such energy, it's hard not to get excited about tasting it. When

he talks about the wine, he also shares stories of where he first tried it and what his memories are. It puts a smile on my face because I share this love of telling stories as well. I'm also as outgoing as he is, so it's easy to see why we're so close. Right before the holiday, he finished building a 500-bottle wine cellar in his basement, so I knew we were going to be quite warm and fuzzy.

I began the evening with mushroom salad and fruit salsa, and the lobster spring rolls came afterward. The lobster meat blended well with the subtle sweetness of the fruit. The salmon was tender, lightly coated in glaze so as not to take away from the taste of the fish. The mushroom risotto was cooked slowly, painfully, but so worth the wait. It was warm, comforting, and really the perfect complement to the salmon. I was pleased with the turnout and even more so when everyone sang my praises.

After dinner, people made their way to the living room and dozed off or talked quietly. I cleaned the kitchen, and my aunts and mother helped clear the dishes away. I was washing a dish when out of nowhere, a loud sound filled the house. It was as if an operatic soprano were singing in the middle of our living room. It turned out it was my mother's friend,

Janet. She was never trained professionally but had sung for a handful of local Cleveland choirs, did a few musicals, and taught young students to sing. Her voice was so powerful, she could have sung at a loud techno nightclub and still would have been heard by everyone. As the rich, melodic notes rolled off her tongue, another sound slowly crept up to meet it.

It appeared that Tyler, my parent's dog, wasn't accustomed to hearing something so distinguished. As she sang, he began howling. The louder and higher she sang, the louder and higher he howled. Either he hated it, or wanted to join in her in a duet. We definitely got our share of music that memorable evening.

MAPLE-CURED SALMON WITH MAPLE GLAZE
YIELD: 4 SERVINGS

4 (4-6 oz.) portions of salmon fillets, with skins on

salt and pepper

1 cup pure maple syrup

2 tablespoons soy sauce

¼ cup beef broth

1 teaspoon Worcestershire sauce

pinch sugar

Preheat oven to 365 degrees.

Season salmon fillets with salt and pepper, set aside in fridge. In saucepan, add maple syrup, soy, beef broth, Worcestershire, sugar, salt, and pepper. Bring to boil and then turn heat down to medium and cook on simmer for 10–12 minutes.

Brush salmon fillets with maple glaze. Heat large sauté pan with olive oil until smoking hot. Lay salmon fillets in the pan, skin side down. Cook for 3–4 minutes. Pour rest of Maple mixture over salmon to deglaze pan. Gently scrape the bottom of the pan with a wooden spoon to loosen the caramelized juices. Put in oven for 6–8 minutes until salmon is cooked to your desired doneness. Take out and let rest 1–2 minutes.

SCORE TIP:

MAPLE-CURED SALMON WITH MAPLE GLAZE

When buying salmon, the best kind to buy is labeled "wild" or "wild caught." Salmon that is labeled "farm raised" is generally full of growth hormones and other chemicals that you do not want to eat. The farm-raised salmon does not provide the benefits of omega 3 fatty acids that wild-caught salmon has. The pink color of farm-raised salmon is artificial. Wild salmon, on the other hand, produce this color naturally. If you see "organic" salmon in your local market, don't assume the salmon is organic. In all honesty, there are no standards and guidelines set for fish labeled "organic", so you have no idea whether the fish is wild caught or farm raised. If you see "organic" salmon at your local market, ask your fishmonger where the salmon came from.

What is the term deglaze mean? In cooking terminology, it mean to add liquid to a hot pan in which foods have been sautéed or roasted in order to dissolve the caramelized goodness that has stuck to the bottom of the pan. So why deglaze? Well the purpose of deglazing is to make a quick sauce and to incorporate some of that flavor of the food that has been left behind, so that flavor can come through in the sauce.

WILD MUSHROOM RISOTTO

YIELD: 4 SERVINGS

2 tablespoon olive oil

1 teaspoon garlic, minced

½ cup yellow onion, diced small

¼ cup green onions, chopped

2½ cups white, cremini and shiitake mushrooms, stems removed, chopped

1 lb. risotto rice

1½ quarts hot chicken stock, as needed

¼ cup white wine

¼ cup Parmesan cheese

1 tablespoon butter

salt and pepper to taste

GARNISH

olive oil

To make risotto: heat medium pot with olive oil. Add garlic, yellow onions and green onions. Cook for 2–3 minutes. Add mushrooms. Cook for 8–10 minutes on medium heat, until onions are translucent and mushrooms are soft. Add rice and incorporate all ingredients. Cook until rice is slightly toasted, about 6–8 minutes. Add hot chicken stock in increments, a few ladles at a time continually stirring. When risotto has absorbed liquid, add a little bit more, continually adding liquid in increments. When risotto is almost done (al dente), add wine. Finish risotto. Add Parmesan cheese and butter. Mix for 2 minutes. Turn off heat. Drizzle with olive oil.

LOBSTER SPRING ROLLS WITH MANGO-PINEAPPLE CHUTNEY

YIELD: 6–8 SERVINGS

1½ cups cooked lobster meat, chopped

½ cup imitation crab meat sticks, diced small

1 tablespoon olive oil

⅓ cup leeks, chopped

½ cup red peppers, diced small

1 tablespoon shallots, minced

1 teaspoon garlic, minced

¼ cup green onions, chopped

¼ cup white wine

1 cup Gruyère cheese, shredded

1 lemon, juiced

½ teaspoon dry thyme, chopped

2 teaspoons fresh sage, chopped

1 tablespoon fresh basil, chopped

canola oil for frying

flour tortillas, small

1 egg, beaten

GARNISH

thick balsamic syrup (optional)

In medium sauté pan on medium-high heat, place olive oil. Add leeks, shallots, garlic, green onions, and peppers. Cook for 10 minutes. Add white wine and cook until mixture is dry. Put into small bowl to cool. In medium bowl, place lobster meat and fake crab meat. Add cheese, herbs, cooled onion mixture, lemon juice, salt, and pepper. Mix together.

Crack egg into small bowl. Add 1 tablespoon water and whisk. Place 2½–3 tablespoons lobster mixture on edge of tortilla and roll up like a burrito. Seal edges of flour tortilla with egg wash. Repeat until lobster mixture is gone.

Place rolls in freezer for 3–4 hours or overnight

In a large, deep skillet, heat 2 inches oil to 375 degrees. Take rolls out of freezer and let sit for 30 minutes before frying. Fry 3–4 at a time until golden brown. Drain on paper towel and season with salt and pepper. Repeat.

Place on baking sheet and bake in oven for 15–22 minutes on 350 degrees.

MANGO-PINEAPPLE CHUTNEY

1 mango, skin removed and diced small

1 small pineapple, top and bottom remove, skin peeled and diced small

1 red pepper, chopped

1 small red onion, diced small

¼ cup apple cider vinegar

⅓ cup brown sugar

1 tablespoon balsamic vinegar

1 tablespoon jalapeño, white pith and seeds removed, minced

2 tablespoons olive oil or canola oil

salt and pepper to taste

¼ teaspoon red pepper flakes

pinch sugar

In a medium sauce pan on high heat, add all ingredients. Incorporate and bring to boil. Then lower heat to medium-low and cook for 40–45 minutes. Take off heat and allow to cool. Serve with lobster rolls. Garnish plate with drizzle of balsamic syrup.

LOBSTER SPRING ROLLS WITH MANGO-PINEAPPLE CHUTNEY

If Gruyère cheese is too expensive, isn't on your list of favorite cheeses, or you can't find it in your local market, here are some recommendations for some substitutes, but first here's the 411 on this amazing cheese.

Gruyère is one of the most famous Swiss Cheeses and Switzerland's most popular cheese. It has a variety of flavor profiles, depending on how long the cheese was aged. When it is young, it has a creamy, sweet, nutty flavor. As it ages, it takes on a more assertive, full forward, earthy taste. The majority of Gruyère cheeses have been aged for eight to eleven months. This long aging time benefits the cheese's melting capacity.

Gruyère is the signature cheese used in French onion soup, chicken cordon bleu, quiches, and fondues. Its high cream content and dense texture makes it the perfect cheese to use in these dishes.

Substitutes for Gruyère: Swiss or Jarlsberg cheese is your best bet. For those who may be put off by the pungent flavor of Gruyère, Jarlsberg is a good alternative for its melting properties.

wild mushroom salad with mesclun-frisée mix, lemon vinaigrette, and blue cheese balls

WILD MUSHROOM SALAD WITH MESCLUN-FRISÉE MIX, LEMON VINAIGRETTE, AND BLUE CHEESE BALLS

YIELD: 4 SERVINGS

MUSHROOM MIXTURE

1 tablespoon olive oil

1 teaspoon garlic, minced

1 tablespoon shallots, minced

6 cups mushrooms, (cremini, shiitake and white button, stems removed, chopped)

1 tablespoon fresh sage, chopped

1 teaspoon fresh thyme, chopped

salt and pepper

½ cup white wine

2 regular-sized bags prewashed mesclun greens with frisée (Earthbound Farms makes a great mix)

LEMON VINAIGRETTE

1 lemon, squeezed

¼ cup orange juice

¼ cup apple cider vinegar

1 teaspoon yellow mustard

pinch sugar

1 teaspoon fresh thyme, chopped

salt and pepper

½ cup olive oil

½ lb. blue cheese, rolled into small balls

In large sauté pan, heat olive oil on medium-high. Add garlic and shallots and cook for 4–5 minutes, lowering heat to medium. Add mushrooms and cook for another 8–10 minutes. Add white wine in increments throughout the cooking process. Cook until all mushrooms are soft and there is minimal liquid in the pan. Add herbs and turn off heat. Salt and pepper to taste

Spoon out onto plates to cool. When cooled completely, put in fridge for several hours.

To make vinaigrette: in small bowl, squeeze lemon. Add orange juice, apple cider vinegar, mustard, herbs, and sugar. Mix together. Whisk olive oil in slowly.

Take mushroom mixture and add ⅓ cup of lemon vinaigrette. Mix together. Set aside.

Center circular mold on plate. Fill with ½ cup mushroom mixture. Pack down lightly. Remove ring mold. (If you do not have a mold, place mushroom mixture neatly in center of plate.)

Combine both lettuces in a bowl. Add remaining dressing, salt, and pepper and toss together. Place on top of each mushroom mixture. Serve cold. Garnish with blue cheese balls.

SCORE TIP:

WILD MUSHROOM SALAD WITH MESCLUN-FRISÉE MIX, LEMON VINAIGRETTE, AND BLUE CHEESE BALLS

Sometimes, shiitakes can be a bit overpowering and you have to like the earthiness taste of mushrooms to like these mushrooms. Shiitakes are prevalent in a lot of Asian dishes and they add a nice "umami" flavor to your palette. If you never heard this term, it has recently been added to the taste profile: salty, sweet, sour, bitter, and—the fifth taste—umami. In English this means, "meaty or savory." The Japanese word literally means, "delicious flavor." Now let me put my science hat on. Umami is a savory taste imparted by glutamate, a type of amino acid, which occurs naturally in many foods. High levels of free glutamate are found in dried seaweed, tomatoes, Parmesan cheese, anchovies, fish sauce, soy sauce, and mushrooms. When mushrooms are grilled, a more intense "umami" flavor becomes prevalent. Now, let's put my chef hat on. Shiitakes are great in soups, stir-fries, salads, casseroles, burgers, and pizza.

CHUNKY FRUIT SOUP INFUSED WITH GINGER-LEMON SYRUP

YIELD: 4–6 SERVINGS

1 pineapple, top and bottom removed, skin peeled, core removed, diced small

1 papaya, peeled, core and seeds removed, diced small

1 mango, peeled, core removed, diced small

1 cup strawberries, diced small

2 kiwis, peeled, diced small

1 cup red grapes, halved

2 tablespoons sugar

GINGER-LEMON SYRUP

2 cups sugar

2 cups water

4 lemon slices

2 tablespoons fresh ginger, chopped

1 tablespoon fresh mint, chopped

mango sorbet

GARNISH

mint leaves

Cut all fruit into bite-sized pieces and put into large bowl. Sprinkle sugar over fruit and mix together. Refrigerate for 1 hour.

In medium saucepan, bring sugar and water to a boil and dissolve sugar. Add lemon slices, ginger, and mint. Turn off heat and let steep for 30 minutes. Cool in fridge.

In dessert bowls, scoop mango sorbet and place in center. Add ¼ cup syrup mixture over sorbet. Add ½–⅔ cup fruit mixture. Garnish with mint.

SCORE TIP:

CHUNKY FRUIT SOUP INFUSED WITH GINGER-LEMON SYRUP

Leftover fruit from this recipe? Make fruit cubes. Take an empty ice cube tray and fill with your leftover fruit from this recipe. Pour a little water over the fruit until it comes to the top of the tray and freeze. These fruit cubes are great in a white wine cocktail, sangria, champagne cocktails, lemonade, orange juice, and grape juice. It's also a great way to get your kids or your stubborn significant other, who hates health food, to eat fruit.

Chef Symon and...

Stoker Spinach Salad with Warm Bacon Dressing, Caramelized Red Onion Bits, and a Fried Egg

This recipe was inspired by Chef Michael Symon, one of the best chefs around. A fellow CIA grad, Michael Symon was the first chef I became intrigued with because of his unique sense of food preparation, types of ingredients he used, and his dynamic, down-to-earth personality. I had the pleasure of meeting Chef Symon at one of his restaurants seven years ago. Lola was his first restaurant in Cleveland before he moved it to East 4th Street. He turned the old Lola into Lolita and created a unique neighborhood boutique café. The original Lola was opened in the Tremont area, which was right on the cusp of downtown Cleveland. Tremont at the time was a quiet, blue-collar, no-frills kind of place when Chef Symon set up shop. He had a presence about him and started to gain a reputation for his outstanding, off-the-wall kind of food. His popularity and food brought in other talented chefs, which sparked the opening of an unprecedented number of outstanding restaurants in the area. Each and every chef owner

Original photo

original recipe photo

had a uniqueness about his cuisine and Tremont started to become the "place to be" on a Friday night. They say Chef Symon is credited for "saving the restaurant scene" in Cleveland and putting it on the map as a place where good food is found.

After I graduated from the CIA in August, I was about to start my fellowship in one of the restaurants on the campus. I had a few weeks off before I started and I flew back to Cleveland to see my family. My parents had already been to Lola and were excited to take me there. We gather up my aunt and uncle to join us and all five of us headed to Lola. It was a night-and-day experience since I had begun culinary training. My palate had changed so dramatically that I was excited to experience Chef Symon's food. As we sat down, I took it all in. The décor was very inviting, dark yet modern, sleek, and fun. Not more than ten minutes after we sat at the table and ordered vino, Chef Symon made his way to our table. I couldn't believe he was actually out and about trolling around the dining room talking to his guests. He had such an inviting, warm, down-to-earth personality. He asked us if were enjoying the wine and what we were thinking of ordering. My father said to him, "This is her first time here and she just graduated from the CIA."

"That's awesome, another fellow CIA grad." Chef Symon wore a huge smile. Since Michael was a fellow CIA alum, he started talking about the good-ole days of culinary school and how different it was back then compared to now. He asked if a few of his past chef instructors were still teaching and proceeded to tell us a funny story about one of them. As he told the story, he laughed in a very distinctive way that I could see was getting under my mom's skin. The look on her face expressed, "Please stop laughing; it's making me annoyed." I thought Michael's laugh was cute but it was making my mom uncomfortable because he kept laughing every five seconds. He congratulated me on my graduation, wished me good luck on my fellowship, and made his way to the next table.

After examining and dissecting the menu, I was ready to dive in. Chef Symon's out-of-the-box thinking on food was something that I had never seen. To go above the norm and think outside the box is what separated him from his competition. This really taught me to not just create the normal stuff. Push the limit on food and see where it goes.

The creations on his menu included this amazing charcuterie platter made from every part of the pig that my father, uncle, and I shared. From fresh prosciutto, Soppressata, fresh bone marrow to smear on crusty bread, to crispy pork belly and wild boar carpaccio, this pigapolzza platter would make even a vegan come over to the other side. Also, we all ordered the spinach salad that had a warm bacon dressing with big chunks of crispy, cured, slab bacon. The salad was topped with a large fried egg, caramelized onions, and big thick rustic croutons. Every morsel I put in my mouth was true heaven and I didn't want it to end. I don't know how anyone cannot like bacon. It makes me sad to think there are people out there like this.

After the experience at Chef Symon's restaurant, I looked beyond the norm of everyday ingredients. He really inspired me to think outside the box when it comes to food preparation because there is a whole world out there to explore beyond everyday dishes. The confidence Chef Symon projects is another thing I admired. A lot of chefs possess a sort of arrogance about them, especially if they become famous. Chef Symon, as big a celebrity chef as he is today, still maintains a down-to-earth, confident, playful personality. I wanted to push the envelope with food just as Chef Symon did and what better guinea pigs to try this out on than my friends and family. I created several recipes in this book that go above and beyond the usual. The first dish I created was the chipotle-cinnamon chicken wings. These two flavors come together like a marriage made in heaven. For another recipe, I used a wild berry wine cooler to marinate chicken. Experiments like this really open up your mind to all sorts of possibilities in the kitchen. That's what memories and experiences are all about. They broaden your horizons and force you to think outside the box.

stoker spinach salad with warm bacon dressing, caramelized red onion bits, and a fried egg

STOKER SPINACH SALAD WITH WARM BACON DRESSING, CARAMELIZED RED ONION BITS, AND A FRIED EGG

YIELD: 4 SERVINGS

2 bags spinach, washed and drained

4 eggs

⅔ cup tomatoes, chopped

1 small red onion, diced small

DRESSING

1 tablespoon olive oil

½ pound bacon, diced small

½ teaspoon chopped fresh garlic

⅓ cup red onion, diced small

⅓ cup apple cider vinegar

1 teaspoon yellow mustard

2 tablespoons balsamic vinegar

1 tablespoon honey

½ cup olive oil

salt and pepper

In medium sauté pan, place a little bit of olive oil on high heat. Add red chopped onions and lower heat to medium-high. Stir often and cook until onions are a nice light caramel color. Cook for 20 minutes. Set aside when done.

In another medium sauté pan, heat olive oil on medium-high. Add garlic and onions and cook for 3–4 minutes. Add bacon and cook bacon until crisp. Take pan off heat and drain 2 tablespoons of bacon grease into small, heat-resistant bowl. Set aside and reserve.

Put bacon pan back on burner on medium heat until pan is hot. Add vinegars, mustard, and honey; stir all ingredients together. Cook for 4–5 minutes to reduce slightly. Turn off heat and whisk oil in slowly to incorporate. Salt and pepper to taste. Let sit for 5 minutes.

In sauté pan, coat with 2 teaspoons of the reserved bacon grease. Heat until smoking hot. Crack eggs and fry on both sides until golden brown.

In large bowl, add spinach and tomatoes, toss with bacon dressing. Put into separate bowls and top each one with caramelized red onion bits and a fried egg. Serve with crusty bread.

SCORE TIP:

STOKER SPINACH SALAD WITH WARM BACON DRESSING, CARAMELIZED RED ONION BITS, AND A FRIED EGG

Pure spinach leaves are filled with a number of essential nutrients, including calcium, folate, iron, magnesium, vitamin C and vitamin A. Although spinach is a great source of iron and calcium, there is a certain compound found in spinach called oxalic acid. This compound blocks the absorption of these two minerals. However, don't start boycotting spinach. There is a way you can easily absorb these important nutrients while enjoying this yummy "lettuce." Pair your spinach with foods high in vitamin C, to aid the absorption of the calcium and iron. Foods to pair your spinach with include tomatoes, orange slices, mandarin slices, mango, papaya, broccoli spears, and red, orange, and yellow peppers.

Thanksgiving and...

Pulled Pork with Bourbon Barbeque Sauce

Cranberry-Vanilla Dressing over Mesclun Greens with Herb, Hazelnut, Goat Cheese Truffles

Pork Tenderloin Stuffed with Bacon, Spinach, and Feta Cheese

Sweet Potato and Sausage Gratin with Savory Maple Glaze

I think the Thanksgiving of 2007 will go down in history as my family's most memorable holiday. Three days before Thanksgiving I started planning a trip to Cleveland—I needed to get away from Connecticut and be with my family. I was done with work and had the next week off. Being a single gal, I didn't want to spend the holiday by myself nor did I want to stay with all the sourpusses in Connecticut. I wanted to give thanks to my family by cooking a nontraditional, gourmet Thanksgiving feast.

Early Wednesday morning, my mother and I headed down to the Cleveland farmers' market, on the West Side. It was a cold morning and the farmers' market was already hopping with last-minute shoppers like us. The Cleveland West Side market is a unique-looking place. It was set up outside in an L shape with all the produce vendors across from one another down a long narrow path. If you walked about five feet from the produce vendors, you'd run into an indoor labyrinth of very small spaces that housed

local vendors selling their amazing products from home-made pierogies, Greek gyros, and homemade pastas to smoked meats, home-made cheese, and many other ethnic foods. On busy weekends in the summer, the market can look like Times Square on New Year's Eve. The produce on display included the most vibrant, lush, and fresh-looking fruits and vegetables I had ever seen. With my tentative grocery list in hand, the sounds of vendors hustling patrons, and the smells of freshly baked breads, warm candied pecans, flowers, and fresh fruit geared me up for the cooking extravaganza. I was so overwhelmed with the amazing local produce that I started to add various things to my list and my mom just shook her head and said, "Are you going to have time to cook all this?"

After a few hours at the market, we had all of our items, and it was go time. I started the prep that day, slicing, dicing, and chopping all the ingredients for my massive feast. My mise-en-place* was coming together and the recipes were coming to fruition with every morsel I chopped. I had a general idea what I was going to cook, but it was very impromptu and I just let my creative juices flow moment to moment. I was halfway through my prep list when I decided to call it a night. Looking around the kitchen, I was going to be up for another hour or more because the mess that I had created looked as if a pack of Tasmanian devils had come through at lightning speed.

Thanksgiving morning came very early; I was up at 6:00 a.m. with a piping hot cup of coffee in hand. I had eight hours until my family and friends arrived. All burners on the stove were going and oven space was becoming very limited. The twenty-five-pound turkey was heading for the oven and since I didn't have any space left, the turducken* was going on the low heated grill outside. My pulled pork was already done from the night before, and I just had to heat it up before the family arrived. I still had my sweet potato and vegetable gratins to cook. My genius mind

came up with a bright idea to move the racks up in the oven so I could squeeze in the two gratins on the bottom rack and the turkey would move to the top. I had my dad help me move the turkey and arrange the racks. Keep in mind that we had a twenty-five-pound turkey in a disposable aluminum pan (not smart). With two hands on each side of the pan, our plan was to lift the turkey out of the oven and move it to the counter so we could arrange the racks, put in the gratins, then the turkey, and we would be back in business. On a count of three, we were to lift the turkey out of the oven.

With our hands firmly gripping both sides, I counted, "One . . . two . . . three." We lifted the turkey out of the oven with an awkward motion, trying not to burn ourselves while we positioned the turkey safely on the counter. But the weight of the turkey and all the juice was too great for the flimsy aluminum pan and the pan won. It seemed to happen in slow motion. The pan buckled, tipped, and spilled grease onto the bottom of the oven. This was not good. The bottom of the oven caught on fire instantly.

Immediately I closed the oven door with the turkey still inside, thinking this would help put out the flames, and my chef brain, for half a second, thought maybe it would give the turkey a little smoke flavor. Oh no! Smoke was pouring out of the oven. I was in a sheer panic and didn't know what to do. As all this was going on, Aunt Carolyn was calmly humming a Monkey's song, "Hey, Hey We're the Monkeys, and People Say We Monkey Around," while she slowly walked over to the kitchen cupboard. As I was about to learn, she was an expert with kitchen fires. She had one every month in her own kitchen. As my panic reached an all-time high, I quickly turned off the oven, opened the door, and smoke flooded my eyes. I couldn't see. The flames were out of control. My father was white as a ghost, walking around very dazed and confused. Not thinking and being extremely panicked, I grabbed my Evian water and threw it on the flames. Let me tell you, when I did this, I think I aged thirty years. Yes, I know, a trained professional chef did the worst thing you could do with a grease fire. I know. The flames started shooting out of the oven at an accelerated rate. Our security alarm system started going off and automatically called the security company. My firefighter aunt grabbed the baking soda out of the cabinet, walked slowly back over to the oven, still humming, carefully opened the oven door, fanning the smoke with her hand, and sprinkled the baking soda over the flames.

The fire was out. The phone started ringing. It was the security company. My somber father answered the phone and told them in a very quiet, stunned voice that everything was under control; we had had a small oven fire. The guy from the response team said, "Well, sir, you aren't the first to cause an oven fire today."

As the commotion settled, the kitchen looked like a foggy morning on San Francisco Bay. My mom, who was getting ready the whole time this was going on, walked into the aftermath with her big bright-yellow rollers in her hair, looking very perplexed. She probably wondered how her professionally trained chef daughter with a CIA education could cause something like this to happen.

We were all silent except my aunt, who turned to my mom joyfully smiling and said, "We had a small oven fire; no big deal,"

After our nerves settled down, I was ready for a cocktail. When the family arrived, they were all were perplexed by the intense smell of smoke. After explaining to them that I had almost burned down my parents' house, it was time for a Wild Turkey shot. What a Thanksgiving to remember. Oh, and everything came out fantastic. The turkey even had a slightly smoky taste to it.

*Mise en place: (pronounced: meez on plas) A French phrase that was coined by the Culinary Institute of America, to mean "everything in its place. For chefs that refer to this term, it means to have all your ingredients that you will need for your menu ready to go before you start cooking.

*Turducken: A dish consisting of a partially deboned turkey stuffed with a deboned duck, which itself is stuffed with a small deboned chicken. The thoracic cavity of the chicken and the rest of the gaps are stuffed, sometimes with a highly seasoned breadcrumb mixture or sausage meat, although some versions have a different stuffing for each bird (Source: Wikipedia.com)

pulled pork with bourbon barbeque sauce

PULLED PORK WITH BOURBON BARBEQUE SAUCE
YIELD: 6-8 SERVINGS

3-4 lb. pork shoulder

olive oil

SPICE RUB

1 teaspoon garlic salt

1 teaspoon cracked black pepper

⅓ cup dried parsley

pinch ground clove

1 teaspoon chili powder

2 teaspoons dry mustard powder

1 tablespoon brown sugar

2 teaspoons smoked
or sweet paprika

2 teaspoons kosher or sea salt

1 tablespoon dry onion flakes

1 teaspoon red pepper flakes

1 quart chicken stock

½ cup white wine

Mix all spices together in small bowl. Pat all over pork shoulder. Let pork sit for 4–6 hours in fridge. Marinate overnight for a more intense flavor.

Preheat oven to 325 degrees.

Take pork out of fridge. Let pork sit for 20 minutes before putting into oven. Pour chicken stock and wine in pan until stock comes half way up pork. Drizzle olive oil over top of pork. Cover pan and roast for 3–4 hours until meat is fork tender and shreds easily.

Take pork out of pan, place on cutting board, and pull apart with fork. Set aside. Reduce pork juices on high heat until liquid equals 1 cup. Keep pork warm until you serve.

bourbon barbeque sauce

BOURBON BARBEQUE SAUCE

2 tablespoons vegetable oil

1 small red onion, diced small

1 teaspoon garlic, chopped

½ cup bourbon

2 (15 oz.) bottles ketchup

1 cup concentrated pork juice (concentrated stock from the pulled pork braise)

½ cup beef stock

¼ cup molasses

¼ cup brown sugar

¼ cup apple cider vinegar

1 tablespoon Worcestershire sauce

1 teaspoon liquid smoke (optional)

1 teaspoon hot sauce

salt and pepper

pinch red pepper flakes

In medium sauté pan, heat oil on high. Add garlic and red onions. Cook for 5 minutes. Lower heat to medium-high. Add bourbon and cook for 4–5 minutes. Add ketchup, molasses, brown sugar, apple cider vinegar, and Worcestershire sauce.

Incorporate all. Cook for 5–6 minutes. Add pork juice and beef stock and mix together. Cook for 10–15 minutes, and then add the remainder of the ingredients. Let simmer for 30 minutes on low heat.

SCORE TIP:

I just wanted to let you know that the bourbon-barbeque pulled pork turned out great! It was easy and fun to make and our friends really enjoyed it. It was nice and spicy too, which made the beer taste even better.

—Erik Jansen

SCORE TIP:

PULLED PORK WITH BOURBON BARBEQUE SAUCE

Generally the best cut of pork to use for pulled pork is the pork shoulder, which has two cuts called the butt and picnic. The difference between butts and picnics is the bone structure: the butt has a small shoulder-blade bone and the picnic has the front leg bone and joint.

The butt end is always misinterpreted. People think this is the actual butt of the pig. The pork shoulder butt is the upper part of the front shoulder. It is the most popular cut to use in a pulled pork recipe because it has less connective tissue, lots of fat marbling throughout the meat and less bone. The marbling melts slowly throughout the cooking process and bastes the meat as it cooks.

The picnic cut is usually made into smoked hams, but a fresh picnic cut also makes for very juicy, fall-off-the-bone pulled pork. This cut is full of fat and connective tissue that adds moisture and flavor to the meat. The large bone helps hold everything together when the meat is falling off the bone as it cooks. I have heard that the meat closest to the bone is the sweetest, and I certainly think the picnic cut, which has a larger bone, is sweeter in taste. But you can be the judge of that. The pork butt is also the preferred cut for pulled pork in barbeque competitions.

cranberry-vanilla dressing over mesclun greens with herb, hazelnut, goat cheese truffles

CRANBERRY-VANILLA DRESSING OVER MESCLUN GREENS WITH HERB, HAZELNUT, GOAT CHEESE TRUFFLES

YIELD: 4 SERVINGS

1 cup of Craisins

½ cup of warm water

2 tablespoons of balsamic vinegar

1 tablespoon sherry vinegar

¼ cup balsamic vinegar

½ vanilla bean, split in half, vanilla removed

salt and pepper

½ cup of olive oil, extra virgin

2 bags mesclun mix or wild greens mix

½ cup chopped hazelnuts, toasted

TRUFFLES

1 small log goat cheese

1 ½ teaspoons dried thyme

2 tablespoons dried parsley

1 teaspoon dried oregano

½ teaspoon salt

½ teaspoon black pepper

In small bowl, combine cranberries, water, and 2 tablespoons balsamic vinegar. Let sit for 45 minutes to one hour.

Drain off ¼ cup liquid and add the mixture to a blender or food processor. Puree on high for 5–10 seconds. Scrape sides toward bottom. Puree again for 10–15 seconds. Add remaining vinegars and vanilla and puree until smooth. Add olive oil in slowly as blender or food processor is running. Season with salt and pepper to taste. Chill in fridge for several hours.

TRUFFLES: In small bowl, place chopped hazelnuts. In another small bowl, place herbs and combine. Take 2 teaspoons of goat cheese and roll into ball. Roll in herb mixture, shake off excess, and roll in hazelnuts to coat. Repeat until goat cheese is gone. Place on plate and refrigerate for 1 hour.

Mix mesclun greens with dressing. Add truffles to salad. Serve immediately.

SCORE TIP:

CRANBERRY-VANILLA DRESSING OVER MESCLUN GREENS WITH HERB, HAZELNUT, GOAT CHEESE TRUFFLES

If you can't find vanilla beans in the store, use a pure vanilla extract.

Pure vanilla extract is made by steeping and soaking chopped vanilla beans in an alcohol/water solution for a few days before leaving it to age for several months. The FDA requires that pure vanilla extract contain 13.35 oz. vanilla beans per gallon of liquid and 35 percent alcohol/65 percent water. Once you achieve aging success, what is left is a deep brown, fragrant solution. Imitation vanilla is artificially flavored with harsh chemicals that will leave a very bitter taste in your desserts and dishes. I would highly recommend going that extra mile, spending a few more bucks, and buying pure vanilla extract. A little bit goes along way.

PORK TENDERLOIN STUFFED WITH BACON, SPINACH, AND FETA CHEESE

YIELD: 6–8 SERVINGS

3–3½ lb. pork tenderloin, lean

salt and pepper

olive oil

½ lb. raw bacon, chopped

1 cup white onions, diced small

1 teaspoon fresh garlic, chopped

4 cups spinach, fresh

¼ teaspoon cinnamon

½ cup feta cheese crumbles

¼ cup cream cheese

⅓ cup Craisins

½ cup chicken stock

¼ cup white wine

Preheat oven to 365 degrees.

Cut pork loin lengthwise, ¾ down, making sure you do not cut through bottom. Open loin like a book (see instructions below). Salt and pepper both sides. Brush with olive oil to coat whole tenderloin.

In medium sauté pan, heat olive oil on medium-high and add bacon. Cook until bacon is crisp. Remove bacon from pan and keep bacon fat in pan. Add onions and garlic to fat and cook for 3–4 minutes until onions are translucent and light brown. Add spinach and allow to wilt down. Add cinnamon and Craisins. Cook mixture until dry. Add bacon to spinach mixture and incorporate other ingredients.

Take tenderloin bottom half and spread cream cheese over the whole tenderloin. Sprinkle feta cheese crumbles on top of cream cheese. Top with spinach mixture. Tie with butcher's twine to hold together. Put in baking pan and add stock and wine to bottom of pan. Place loin in pan and put in over for 1 hour. Take temperature and pull at 155 degrees. Allow to cool and slice into medallions.

SCORE TIP:

PORK TENDERLOIN STUFFED WITH BACON, SPINACH, AND FETA CHEESE

How to butterfly pork tenderloin: Lay tenderloin on flat surface, preferably a cutting board. Place one hand on top of the tenderloin to hold it. With a sharp knife, start cutting a horizontal incision, about an inch deep at the top end of the loin an inch up from cutting board. As you make your way down the loin, pull back the meat.

Once the entire length of the loin is cut, return to the top and cut deeper into the loin. Follow the same procedure as above and continue to cut no more than an inch into the loin as you make your way down each time.

Continue this until the entire loin lies flat across your cutting board like a piece of paper. Now you're ready to stuff your loin.

SWEET POTATO AND SAUSAGE GRATIN WITH SAVORY MAPLE GLAZE

YIELD: 4–6 SERVINGS

1 lb. sweet Italian sausages, casings removed

1¼ cups chicken stock

1 cup dry white wine

¼ cup orange marmalade jam

½ cup real maple syrup

2 tablespoons butter

2¼ cups sliced leeks

¾ cup yellow onion, chopped

3 lb. sweet potatoes, peeled and thinly sliced in circles

2 tablespoons fresh sage leaves, chopped

1 tablespoon fennel seed

1 cup Parmesan cheese

Preheat oven to 400 degrees.

In large skillet over medium-high heat, cook sausages thoroughly, about 7–10 minutes. Take out sausages and put on plate. In same skillet, add stock, wine, marmalade, maple syrup, and butter. Bring liquid mixture to boil and reduce to 1½ cups. Pour liquid into another bowl and reserve. In the same skillet, add olive oil on medium-high heat. Add leeks, fennel seeds, and onions, and sauté until soft, about 7–9 minutes.

In a large baking dish, shingle potato slices to cover the entire surface. Sprinkle some of the sausage, cheese, and leek mixture over all. Sprinkle a little bit of the sage over all toppings. Keep layering ingredients and repeat above steps. Pour broth mixture over entire gratin. Sprinkle with remaining Parmesan cheese. Cover and bake for 20–22 minutes. Uncover and bake until potatoes are golden brown and tender and liquid thickens, about 10–15 more minutes. Take out of oven and let sit for 2 minutes before serving.

SCORE TIP:

SWEET POTATO AND SAUSAGE GRATIN WITH SAVORY MAPLE GLAZE

There are 101 ways to slice a potato. In this recipe you have several options. You can do it the old-fashioned way by slicing the potatoes with a very sharp knife into · inch circles. Another option you have—and you probably didn't know you had this on hand—is a box cheese grater. The old-fashioned kind has four sides with various grating options. The majority of graters have a slicing option. The potatoes will come out a little thinner than they would when sliced by hand, but that will work for this recipe.

pesto fusilli with potatoes, green beans, and peas, with shaved parmesan cheese

The Italian Way and...

Toasted Crostini Topped with Prosciutto and Honey, with Goat Cheese-Mascarpone Whip

Fruit Salad with Bean Sprouts and Radicchio, Drizzled with Honey

Pesto Fusilli with Potatoes, Green Beans, and Peas, with Shaved Parmesan Cheese

A few years ago on a family trip to the Lago di Coma (Lake Coma) region of Italy, I realized how good Italian cuisine really is. With every morsel of food that I ate and enjoyed, I felt like a child eating something really good for the very first time. I had never tasted pure, simple food the way I did when I was in Italy. The Italians truly know how to live life and how to prepare unbelievable food. The recipes are very simple, with minimal ingredients, and every morsel that danced across my taste buds on that trip were out of this world. It was a very special trip for me because I went with a lot of my family and it was great to spend the week with my parents. If it had not been for them, I would not have had the opportunity to go on the trip.

The Italian way of life, in which wonderful, simple food is enjoyed and life is celebrated every day, is something that Americans should instill in their lives. This is why I wrote this cookbook—all my recipes symbolize the true meaning of life and I have created memories for years to come. As the Italians say, nothing brings them more happiness than when family and friends get together for a meal. When they cook, the whole family is involved from start to finish. Everyone has a job to do in the kitchen and they prepare their food with great pride and love. They use the most simple, natural, amazing ingredients, and when these ingredients are combined, they taste like nothing you have ever tasted before. The food is truly heavenly. When I think about my experience in Italy and what life should be about, I am truly blessed for the family and friends I have. This proves my theory that food, family, and friends go hand and hand and bring great memories. Eating well feeds the soul.

TOASTED CROSTINI TOPPED WITH PROSCIUTTO AND HONEY, WITH GOAT CHEESE-MASCARPONE WHIP

YIELD: 4 – 6 SERVINGS

1 baguette, sliced in ·-inch circles

olive oil

1 small log goat cheese

½ cup mascarpone cheese

¼ teaspoon garlic salt

½ teaspoon dried oregano

1 tablespoon olive oil

½ lb. prosciutto, thinly sliced

GARNISH

honey

Preheat oven to 365 degrees.

Take bread circles, brush with olive oil, and lay on baking sheet. Season with salt and pepper. Bake until light golden brown.

In small bowl, place goat cheese mascarpone, garlic salt, oregano, and olive oil. Mix until all ingredients are incorporated. Take 1 tablespoon cheese mixture and frost each bread circle. Top with thin slice of prosciutto. Repeat these steps until all bread circles are complete. Drizzle honey over each piece. Serve.

SCORE TIP:

TOASTED CROSTINI TOPPED WITH PROSCIUTTO AND HONEY, WITH GOAT CHEESE-MASCARPONE WHIP

The flavor combination in these Italian delights will blow your taste buds to the next level. If you're having a hard time finding mascarpone cheese, substitute cream cheese.

FRUIT SALAD WITH BEAN SPROUTS AND RADICCHIO, DRIZZLED WITH HONEY

YIELD: 4 SERVINGS

2 kiwis, peeled, diced small

½ cantaloupe, peeled, diced small

1 cup blueberries

½ melon, peeled, diced small

2 oranges, peeled, chopped

2 peaches, halved, pits removed, diced small

½ cup shredded purple radicchio (or red cabbage)

1 cup bean sprouts

honey

GARNISH

yogurt (optional)

In large bowl, add all ingredients except honey. Mix together very well.

Put salad in bowls and drizzle with honey. Garnish with a small side of plain or vanilla yogurt. Serve chilled.

PESTO FUSILLI WITH POTATOES, GREEN BEANS, AND PEAS, WITH SHAVED PARMESAN CHEESE

YIELD: 4 SERVINGS

1 lb. fusilli pasta, dry

2 cups cooked potatoes, quartered (you can use tricolored potatoes, blue potatoes, Yukon gold and/or red potatoes)

1½ cups fresh green beans, cooked, cut into bite- sized pieces

½ cup cooked peas

1 small jar of pesto sauce (⅓ – ½ cup)

¼ cup olive oil

⅓–½ cup chicken stock

¼ cup Parmesan cheese

salt and pepper

GARNISH

shaved Parmesan cheese

truffle oil (optional)

Cook pasta according to package instructions. Drain pasta and put back into pot.

Heat pot with pasta, on medium-high heat. Add olive oil, pesto and chicken stock. Mix together.

Add all other ingredients, incorporate and lower heat to medium. Cook for 10–12 minutes. Season with salt and pepper to taste.

If sauce is too thick, thin out with more chicken stock. Garnish with Parmesan cheese and a drizzle of truffle oil.

SCORE TIP:

PESTO FUSILLI WITH POTATOES, GREEN BEANS, AND PEAS, WITH SHAVED PARMESAN CHEESE

I had never eaten pasta and potatoes combined together in one dish before. I discovered this dish in a very small town outside Lake Como, Italy. We literally stumbled upon this restaurant in the middle of a vineyard that was getting ready to close for the harvest season. The vineyard parking lot was empty—not a single car or soul around. We thought the restaurant was closed, and we were getting back into our cars when the owner came running out, screaming to us in Italian. He spoke a little English (thank God!), and invited us into his restaurant for lunch. As we walked into the desolate restaurant, I thought I had stepped into *Alice in Wonderland* meets a Salvador Dali painting. It was very surreal, but we were treated like family. I had never tried so many new, unique dishes, and this particular dish made a lasting impression on me. I will never forget that culinary experience.

Chapter 5

Happy Endings

RECIPES FREE OF DAIRY AND GLUTEN: HEALTHY RECIPES SO DELICIOUS THAT YOU WON'T EVEN MISS THE UNHEALTHY INGREDIENTS

Mock Brown Rice Risotto with Wild Mushrooms and Garbanzo Beans

Grilled Flatbread with White Bean Puree, Sun-Dried Tomato Spread, and Thai Cucumber-Mint Salad

Roasted Butternut Squash Soup with Eggplant Puree

Grilled Vegetable Gratin with Roasted Butternut Squash Puree and Asian Pesto Puree

Deviled Eggs with Roasted Red Pepper Hummus Filling

Asparagus Guacamole

Free-of-Gluten Crispy Chicken with Pesto, Brown Rice Pasta, and Asian vegetables

After being diagnosed with a food intolerance, I viewed food preparation in a whole new way. I just never "felt right" in culinary school, and my diagnosis showed me the secret behind the mystery.

Being a chef and unable to tolerate any dairy products is the most horrible thing in the world. Well, in my mind it is. In today's society, everyone associates foods that are prepared with butter, heavy cream, and high-fat dairy products with indulgence and a taste that's off the charts. On the other hand, when people hear that certain dishes are prepared with tofu, olive oils, spices, and healthier ingredients, they assume they're not going to taste as good and they'll be dissatisfied.

I have come up with various ways to incorporate nondairy ingredients into dishes that would normally call for high-fat, unhealthy dairy ingredients. These recipes get right down to the basics—the ingredients we were born to eat and love. These fresh, natural foods are the raw ingredients of life. The dishes were created without the heavy, unhealthy fillers that are normally found in traditional preparations. When you prepare and taste these dishes, you won't miss a thing—trust me!

First, a note about dairy-free ingredient alternatives:

SILKEN TOFU: This ingredient, whether you're a vegan, have a dairy allergy/intolerance, or need to reduce your fat and calories, is a great replacement for sour cream or heavy cream. Blend drained silken tofu with olive oil, balsamic vinegar, and fresh herbs and you've got yourself a great, dairy-free, healthy replacement. I use this technique in several of my recipes listed in this cookbook.

VINEGARS: If you are on sodium-restricted diet or just need to watch your sodium intake, try adding various flavored vinegars to your recipes. Vinegar has minimal calories and is virtually sodium free. When you eat something that has vinegar in it, your mouth starts to salivate and you crave more. Vinegar can also calm any salt craving because of its acidic properties and salty taste. The majority of pure vinegars have minimal sodium levels.

BETTER THAN CREAM CHEESE: This product is amazingly dairy free. It's very creamy in texture and tastes a lot like real cream cheese. I add this to a lot of my dishes in place of butter, sour cream, real cream cheese, and regular cream. It really gives my dishes body, depth, and richness.

CAULIFLOWER: It's a love–hate relationship with cauliflower; you either love it or hate it. But if you're not a fan of this versatile veggie, I will change your mind and you will fall in love. There is a great way to make cauliflower into what I call fake mashed potatoes. If you're watching your calories or carbs, this is a perfect side to help feed your fatty fix. Cut the cauliflower up into pieces and put into a pot of boiling salted water. Boil for 8–10 minutes and drain in colander. In food processor or blender, add cooked cauliflower, ¼ cup olive oil, 1 tablespoon cream cheese (omit if you have a dairy allergy), salt and pepper to taste. Blend until very smooth. If you want to get really fancy, sauté some chopped leeks until golden brown and crisp and add that into your pureed delight.

MOCK BROWN RICE RISOTTO WITH WILD MUSHROOMS AND GARBANZO BEANS

YIELD: 4–6 SERVINGS

½ block silken tofu, drained

¼ cup balsamic vinegar

2 tablespoons olive oil

½ teaspoon garlic salt

¼ teaspoon ground black pepper

salt

1 quart chicken stock, hot

(vegetable stock can be used)

1 cup white wine (the rest you can drink)

2 tablespoons olive oil

1 small yellow onion, diced small

1 teaspoon garlic, minced

⅓ cup green onions, chopped

½ cup red peppers, chopped

1½ cups portabella mushrooms, stems removed, chopped

2 cups raw brown rice

1 tablespoon chives, chopped

1 tablespoon parsley, chopped

1 (15 oz.) can garbanzo beans, drained

Cut tofu and place in blender. Add balsamic, olive oil, garlic salt, and black pepper. Blend until very smooth. Season to taste with salt. Reserve and set aside in fridge. In medium saucepan, place chicken stock and wine. Bring to boil and then turn down heat. Place lid on pot and simmer on low.

In medium stockpot, heat olive oil on high. Add onion, green onions, garlic, and red peppers. Lower temperature to medium-high and cook for 5–7 minutes. Add mushrooms. Cook for another 7–9 minutes. Add rice and make sure to incorporate all ingredients. Cook until rice is slightly toasted, about 6–8 minutes. Add hot chicken stock mixture in increments, continually stirring. When rice has absorbed liquid, add a little bit more and continue to add liquid in increments. When rice is almost done (al dente), add a couple splashes of wine. Add herbs and beans to rice mixture. Add whipped tofu mixture, incorporate all together and turn off heat. Season with salt and pepper. Serve in bowls. Garnish with fresh herbs.

SCORE TIP:

MOCK BROWN RICE RISOTTO WITH WILD MUSHROOMS AND GARBANZO BEANS

You have to taste it to believe it is the theme for this recipe. I know, I know. Some of you are already scared off by the first ingredient listed: tofu. It's not that bad an ingredient and there are so many things you can do with tofu. It doesn't have to taste as if you're eating a piece of soggy bread. Tofu is a great source of calcium, protein, and iron. In this recipe, I blend the you-know-what out of it and mix it with a few other ingredients to create a sour-cream-like substitute. In the risotto recipe, this creates that creamy, rich, dairy "mouth feel" that is associated with risotto. I tried this recipe out on a few friends and I didn't tell them I had used tofu in place of the butter and cheese. They couldn't believe how yummy this risotto was. See, everyone, you gotta taste it to believe it. I wouldn't lie.

grilled flatbread with white bean puree, sun-dried tomato spread, and thai cucumber-mint salad

GRILLED FLATBREAD WITH WHITE BEAN PUREE, SUN-DRIED TOMATO SPREAD, AND THAI CUCUMBER-MINT SALAD

YIELD: 6–8 SERVINGS

WHITE BEAN PUREE

2 (15 oz.) cans white beans, slightly drained

1 teaspoon garlic, chopped

½ – ¾ cup olive oil

1½ teaspoon lemon juice

1 teaspoon fresh chopped thyme

1 teaspoon chopped rosemary

salt and ground pepper

SUN-DRIED TOMATO CHUTNEY

¾ cup sun-dried tomatoes, packed in oil, chopped

2 tablespoons olive oil

1 tablespoon balsamic vinegar

1 teaspoon honey

1 tablespoon chopped flat-leaf parsley

flatbread or pita

Puree the beans, garlic, olive oil, lemon juice, and thyme in food processor until smooth. Season with salt and pepper. Set aside.

In small bowl, mix together tomatoes, olive oil, vinegar, honey, and parsley, and season with salt and pepper to taste.

Preheat grill to 325 degrees.

Brush flatbread or pita with olive oil top and bottom. Grill on both sides until golden with grill marks, about 1–2 minutes. Remove from grill and spread each flatbread with thin layer of white bean puree and tomato chutney. Top with Thai salsa. Repeat with each flatbread/pita piece.

THAI CUCUMBER-MINT SALAD

1 large seedless cucumber, diced small

¼ cup green onion, chopped

½ cup radish, thinly sliced

¼ cup mint leaves, chopped

1 tablespoon fresh parsley, chopped

DRESSING

1 teaspoon fresh ginger, finely chopped

1 lime, squeezed

¼ cup rice wine or apple cider vinegar

1 teaspoon sugar

1 tablespoon olive oil

salt and pepper

In small bowl, mix all dressing ingredients well until they come together. Season with salt and pepper to taste. Pour dressing mixture over cucumber mixture. Toss until combined.

SCORE TIP:

GRILLED FLATBREAD WITH WHITE BEAN PUREE, SUN-DRIED TOMATO SPREAD, AND THAI CUCUMBER-MINT SALAD

You can make this recipe gluten free by using gluten-free pita or gluten-free flatbread.

If you're pressed for time, you can always make the sun-dried tomato spread and white bean puree a day before, but save the Thai cucumber mint salsa for your day off. It doesn't hold well overnight because the ingredients get a little too mushy and don't taste as fresh.

roasted butternut squash soup with eggplant puree

ROASTED BUTTERNUT SQUASH SOUP WITH EGGPLANT PUREE

YIELD: 4–6 SERVINGS

2 large butternut squashes (or 3 small to medium butternut squashes), peeled, seeded, cut into chunks

½ cup olive oil

salt and pepper to taste

1 medium-sized eggplant, cut into ¼-inch circles

⅓ cup olive oil

⅓ cup balsamic vinegar

salt and pepper to taste

4 cloves garlic

1 package silken tofu, drained

¼ cup olive oil

2 tablespoons balsamic vinegar

2 tablespoons fresh chives, chopped

1 teaspoon hot sauce

½ tablespoon fresh rosemary, chopped

salt and pepper to taste

1 quart chicken stock (or vegetable stock for vegan)

1 tablespoon apple cider vinegar

2 tablespoons fresh chives, chopped

On two baking sheets, spread out butternut squash chunks. Drizzle with olive oil and season with salt and pepper. Toss to coat all of them. On a third sheet, lay slices of eggplant and coat with olive oil and balsamic vinegar. Put garlic cloves on the eggplant sheet. Place all sheets in 375-degree oven and cook for 40–45 minutes. Eggplant might cook faster, so remove when soft and gold brown.

While vegetables are roasting, place tofu, olive oil, vinegar, chives, hot sauce, rosemary, basil, salt, and pepper in food processor or blender. Blend until very smooth. Adjust seasoning to taste. Remove and store in container in fridge.

When eggplant and butternut squash are finished, take out of oven and cool for 10–15 minutes. In food processor, in separate batches, add all eggplant and garlic cloves. Blend until smooth. Remove eggplant puree and put in container. Set aside.

In same food processor, in separate batches, add butternut squash and blend until smooth.

Combine eggplant and butternut squash purees in medium stockpot. Heat pot on medium. Add chicken stock and vinegar. If soup is too thick, add more chicken stock. Bring to boil and then reduce heat to medium-low. Simmer for 35–40 minutes. Turn off heat and add tofu mixture. Mix all together. Top soup with a few dollops of whipped tofu mixture.

SCORE TIP:

ROASTED BUTTERNUT SQUASH SOUP WITH EGGPLANT PUREE

Can I get an amen with this recipe? All sorts of yummy goodness going on in this soup. First and foremost this is another "you gotta taste it to believe it" recipe. I served this to my father of all people. He hates "healthy" food, but he had no idea that this soup was creamless and butterless. Using the trick that I play in the mock risotto recipe, the tofu is blended into a sour-cream consistency with fresh, vibrant herbs, olive oil, and balsamic vinegar. This is then added at the end of the recipe to create that creamy, fatty texture that we all love so much.

This recipe calls for chicken stock, which can be replaced with a good vegetable stock if you want to make the dish vegetarian.

GRILLED VEGETABLE GRATIN WITH ROASTED BUTTERNUT SQUASH PUREE AND ASIAN PESTO PUREE

YIELD: 4–6 SERVINGS

1 medium eggplant, sliced lengthwise into ¼-inch pieces

2 yellow squash, sliced lengthwise into ¼-inch pieces

2 zucchini, sliced lengthwise into ¼-inch pieces

2 red peppers, tops and core removed, sliced in large chunks

2 green peppers, tops and core removed, sliced in large chunks

1 medium red onion, thinly sliced

⅓ cup olive oil

½ cup balsamic vinegar

BUTTERNUT SQUASH PUREE

1 medium butternut squash, peel and seeds removed, cut into chunks

¼ cup olive oil

½ cup vegetable stock

2 tablespoons balsamic vinegar

sea salt

Asian Pesto

1 cup fresh basil leaves

⅓ cup fresh mint

¼ cup fresh parsley

1 teaspoon fresh garlic, chopped

2 teaspoons fresh ginger, chopped

1 cup unsalted peanuts

½ cup olive oil

½ teaspoon sesame oil (optional)

Optional: gluten-free bread crumbs or regular bread crumbs, salt and pepper

---

Preheat oven to 375 degrees.

On baking sheet, add all vegetables. Brush with olive oil and drizzle balsamic vinegar over them. Season with salt and pepper. Bake for 25–30 minutes until al dente. Take out of oven and allow to cool.

To make butternut squash: place chunks of butternut squash on a baking sheet. Toss with olive oil and season with salt and pepper. Bake for 35–40 minutes until squash is very soft. Take out of oven and allow to cool. Combine butternut squash, vinegar, and vegetable stock in a food processor. Blend until smooth. Season with salt and pepper. Set aside.

To make Asian pesto: add basil leaves, mint, parsley, garlic, ginger, and peanuts to food processor. Blend until it forms a paste. While food processor is on, drizzle in olive oil very slowly until mixture is smooth. Set aside.

Layer bottom of baking dish with vegetables. Take ⅔ cup butternut squash puree and spread over vegetables. Add another layer of vegetables. Top with ¼ cup Asian pesto. Spread evenly. Alternate these steps until vegetables are gone. Top with butternut squash. Bake for 40–45 minutes. Allow to cool for several minutes before cutting.

SCORE TIP:

GRILLED VEGETABLE GRATIN WITH ROASTED BUTTERNUT SQUASH PUREE AND ASIAN PESTO PUREE

Gratin is a fancy French culinary technique meaning a thin layer of bread crumbs, butter, and sometimes cheese is heated under a broiler or in the oven until the top is brown and crisp. In this recipe I eliminate the butter and cheese and replace them with flavorful pesto and butternut squash. You can use regular bread crumbs, but if you want the dish to be gluten free, you must use gluten-free bread crumbs. This texture really adds to this dish and is a nice accompaniment to all the layers of flavors. A great dish to impress your guests.

NOTE: A great cheese to add is Parmesan or Asiago cheese. Sprinkle this on top of the gratin along with the bread crumbs to create a cheesy, veggie delight.

Believe it or not, hummus with eggs is out of this world. I first discovered this one morning when I was attending my breakfast cookery class at culinary school. One can only imagine how anyone could think at 3:00 a.m. when the class started, but my brain was already raring because of what I had to go through to get there that morning. At school, it was extremely rare for classes to be canceled due to inclement weather. I lived in upstate New York where they get their fair share of snow. We had a strict policy about missing/skipping classes. If you missed more than two days per year, you automatically failed that particular class and you would have to retake it. One fine day in January, at 2:00 a.m., I woke up to two feet of snow and my car was buried. I had less than thirty minutes to dig my car out and drive five miles to school in the snowy mess. Classes were still on and I was stressed out beyond words as to how the hell I was going to get to school. With minimal snow-removal tools, I took a broom and started sweeping the snow off my car. The snow around my tires was a different story. It was so compacted, I now dug with my hands to free the tires and create a path so I could back out. What a mess, I thought. There was no way I was getting out. I climbed into my car and tried to back out to no avail. My tires spun and went nowhere. Almost in tears, covered from head to toe in snow in my chef outfit, I thought it was hopeless; I was not going to get to class. I took one last shot at backing my car out of the snowy tomb. It was all or nothing. With one foot to the gas, I gunned it and spun my tires. All of sudden I felt my car roll back. Success! I was on my way to school.

DEVILED EGGS WITH ROASTED RED PEPPER HUMMUS FILLING

YIELD: 6–8 SERVINGS

6 eggs, hard boiled, shells removed

¾ cup roasted red pepper hummus

1 teaspoon balsamic vinegar

1 teaspoon olive oil

½ teaspoon lemon juice

1 tablespoon fresh chives, chopped

¼ cup roasted red peppers, chopped

salt and pepper

Cut hard boiled eggs in half. Removed yolk, put into bowl, and reserve. To yolk bowl add the rest of ingredients, except chives and roasted red peppers. Mix together until all ingredients are incorporated. Season with salt and pepper. Fill each egg with hummus mixture. Top egg with chives and roasted red peppers for garnish. Refrigerate for an hour before serving.

SCORE TIP:

DEVILED EGGS WITH ROASTED RED PEPPER HUMMUS FILLING

Using hummus is great way to reduce calories and fat and you will not suffer on taste. There is tons of flavored hummus on the market today and any of those will work in this recipe.

asparagus guacamole

ASPARAGUS GUACAMOLE

YIELD: 4 SERVINGS

2 full bunches asparagus, fibrous stems removed

1 medium avocado, diced small

½ medium red onion, diced small

1 jalapeño, white pith removed, deseeded, diced small

1 teaspoon garlic, chopped

⅓ cup fresh cilantro, chopped

1 medium tomato, diced small

1 lime, squeezed

2 teaspoons apple cider vinegar

½ teaspoon garlic salt

¼ teaspoon black pepper

1 tablespoon olive oil

salt to taste

Take both bunches of asparagus, remove fibrous ends, and cut into bite-sized pieces. Bring large pot of heavily salted water to a boil and add all asparagus pieces. Have a large bowl of ice water ready to go. Cook asparagus for 6–8 minutes or until very soft. Remove asparagus with slotted spoon and place in ice water. Let cool and then drain in colander. In food processor, add asparagus in batches. Pulse until slightly smooth. Scrape out into bowl and repeat until all asparagus is pureed. Put asparagus mixture in colander for 20 minutes to drain excess water out. In medium bowl, add asparagus mixture and rest of ingredients. Mix together well. Salt and pepper to taste. Refrigerate for several hours before serving. Serve with tortilla chips, crackers, or pita chips.

ASPARAGUS GUACAMOLE

This unique dish is great for individuals who are looking to reduce fat and calories in their diet but not skimp on taste. I have taken a standard dish that people love but don't love what it does to their waistline. Who doesn't love guacamole, right? When you go to your local Mexican joint, it's standard that you order the guacamole with your favorite beverages to start off your evening, right? In this recipe, the guacamole is a lot lighter in texture than regular guacamole. But I guarantee that the taste is amazing and you'll be happy you made it. You can serve this dish with tortilla chips, pita chips, veggies, crackers, or crusty, toasted bread slices. Also, it's great to put in a wrap. When making a turkey wrap, I put some of the guacamole spread on the tortilla, layer it with turkey, tomatoes, and mustard, and roll it up. So yummy.

free-of-gluten crispy chicken with pesto, brown rice pasta, and asian vegetables

FREE-OF-GLUTEN CRISPY CHICKEN WITH PESTO, BROWN RICE PASTA, AND ASIAN VEGETABLES

YIELD: 4 SERVINGS

FREE-OF-GLUTEN CRISPY CHICKEN

1½ cup olive oil

4 chicken breasts, boneless, skinless

⅔ cup gluten-free flour

1 egg, beaten

1 tablespoon water

1 cup gluten-free bread crumbs

½ cup yellow onions, chopped

2 teaspoons fresh dill, chopped

½ lemon, juiced

PASTA

1 lb. brown rice pasta

½ cup pesto sauce (see recipe below or buy ready-made pesto sauce)

½ cup chicken stock

½ cup butternut squash soup (purchase at your local grocery store)

¼ cup sun-dried tomatoes, chopped

1 tablespoon balsamic vinegar

2 tablespoons yellow onions, chopped

2 cups frozen vegetable stir-fry mix

1 tablespoon fresh parsley, chopped

salt

pepper

Preheat oven to 365 degrees.

To bread chicken: Take three medium-sized plates. Place the gluten-free flour on the first plate. Place the beaten egg on the other plate and mix with the water. Put the rice bread crumbs on the third plate. Coat piece of chicken with gluten-free flour; shake off excess. Next, dip chicken in egg wash, and then cover with the rice bread crumbs. Set aside on plate and repeat. Salt and pepper to taste.

Fill medium pot with water and make pasta according to package instructions. Drain and reserve.

In medium sauté pan, heat olive oil on high until very hot. Add chicken and sauté until both sides are golden brown, about 6–8 minutes. Add onions and put entire pan in oven to finish cooking. Cook for 15–25 minutes until chicken is completely cooked.

To make sauce: heat medium saucepan on medium-high. Add sun-dried tomatoes and onions. Sauté for 2–3 minutes. Add pesto, chicken stock, butternut squash soup and balsamic vinegar. Mix all together. Bring to a small boil. If sauce is too thick, thin out with more chicken stock. Add frozen vegetables and cook for 7–8 minutes. Add cooked pasta and parsley and mix all together. Cook for another 4–5 minutes. Serve hot.

PESTO

½ cups toasted pine nuts	¼ cup fresh parsley	⅓ – ½ cup olive oil
1½ cups basil leaves	2 teaspoons garlic, chopped	salt and pepper

In food processor, add all ingredients except for olive oil. Blend until all ingredients are incorporated and smooth. With processor running, add olive oil in slowly. Season to taste with salt and pepper.

SCORE TIP:

FREE-OF-GLUTEN CRISPY CHICKEN WITH PESTO, BROWN RICE PASTA, AND ASIAN VEGETABLES

If you're having a hard time finding gluten-free flour and/or gluten-free bread crumbs, here are few suggestions that might help you.

Gluten-free flour: there are many products out on the market today and they are becoming more prevalent at your local markets. When I first made this recipe, I only had gluten-free pancake mix, so I used that as my flour. It came out really well. So you can use gluten-free pancake mix as an alternative if you don't have gluten-free flour.

If you can't find gluten-free bread crumbs, just buy some gluten-free bread and blend in a blender or food processor until it turns into fine crumbs.

I also tried blending raw brown rice in a food processor until it was finely crumbed. I breaded the chicken with this, but I was nearly scalded when I set the rice-breaded chicken in the hot oil to cook. The rice popped and caused the oil to go everywhere, even on my skin. Not fun. So I don't recommend trying this at home. I wanted to tell you this just in case one of you has a crazy, culinary wild hair and loves to experiment in the kitchen.

Chapter 6

The Sweet Spot

These recipes are not for the faint of heart; you need a seriously sweet tooth to enjoy desserts this tasty. I created them for my father, Joe. He is the biggest foodie I know and a genius when it comes to wines. If he could have it his way, he would retire from the medical profession, open up a food and wine store, and schmooze with the ladies all day long. He would be in his glory.

I am so grateful to have a father like him. He is the most generous, hardworking, honest man I know, and he would do anything for you. He's a passionate gastronome, like me, and we share a passion for good, simple food. I created these amazing desserts with him in mind, and you can guarantee he has given his seal of approval to them. You will not be disappointed. These delicious sweets are great with a tawny port or a nice cup of Joe. No pun intended.

peanut butter and jelly truffles

PEANUT BUTTER AND JELLY TRUFFLES

2 cups whipping cream

21 oz. dark chocolate, chopped in small pieces

1 tablespoon butter, unsalted

½ cup peanut butter, melted in microwave

½ cup berry jam (strawberry, raspberry, or boysenberry)

¼ cup Chambord or any berry liquor

1 teaspoon vanilla extract

1 cup unsweetened cocoa powder

1½ cups shredded coconut

Heat heavy cream in saucepan until bubbles begin to form around the edge of pan. Make sure chocolate is chopped into small pieces so it melts quickly and easily. Place chopped chocolate in medium-sized mixing bowl. Make ganache by pouring about half the hot cream over chocolate and let sit for 30 seconds to melt chocolate. Then slowly whisk until smooth. Do not add all the hot cream to cold chocolate at once. The shock of temperature extremes could cause fat in chocolate to separate. Add remaining cream gradually and mix until all hot cream is incorporated and ganache is smooth. Add melted peanut butter, liquor, and vanilla. Whisk until incorporated and chocolate is melted.

Place in fridge for 2–3 hours until mixture hardens.

Place cocoa in separate bowls. Once mixture hardens, use a melon baller to scoop out quarter-sized truffles. Roll truffles between hands into rounds. Roll truffle in cocoa power. Place on baking sheet. When all truffles are rolled, cover tray with plastic wrap and chill until ready to serve.

SCORE TIP:

PEANUT BUTTER AND JELLY TRUFFLES

Ganache is the foundation for truffles. Ganache is a French term meaning a smooth mixture of chocolate and cream. To make a ganache, as we did in this recipe, chocolate is chopped up into small pieces and hot cream is poured over the chocolate. It's mixed together until all is blended and the chocolate is melted and smooth. Then it is put in the fridge to harden. Truffles are not the only thing a ganache is used for. It's used for frostings, filling in pastries, and candies. The texture of the ganache depends on the ratio of cream to chocolate. The more cream you have, the softer the ganache, which is fairly liquid at room temperature. This is suitable for filling pastries and frosting cakes. A bigger portion of chocolate and less cream creates a ganache that is thick like paste. After several hours in the fridge, this dense chocolate creation is used for truffles. So chill, roll, and go!

LACTOSE-FREE PUMPKIN STRUDEL COOKIES

2 cups all-purpose flour

½ teaspoon ground cinnamon

¼ teaspoon baking powder

¼ teaspoon salt

1 cup soy butter, softened

1¼ cups sugar

1 egg (for vegan, ¼ cup egg replacement)

¼ teaspoon vanilla extract

1 cup canned pumpkin puree

1 teaspoon pumpkin pie spice

¼ cup, plus 1 cup brown sugar

Preheat oven to 375 degrees.

Sift flour, cinnamon, baking powder, and salt together twice. Cream soy butter and sugar in a mixer until light and fluffy. Combine egg, vanilla, and almond extract and add to creamed mixture. Mix on medium speed until combined. Add sifted ingredients and mix only until combined; dough should be stiff.

Roll dough out between two sheets of parchment paper or plastic wrap to a 12-inch by 9-inch rectangle. Make sure that you roll out dough evenly. Place dough in freezer until firm—about 15 minutes.

Mix together the canned pumpkin, pumpkin pie spice, and ¼ cup brown sugar for filling.

Remove dough from freezer and peel back the top parchment paper. Thinly spread the pumpkin filling evenly over the dough.

Starting at one end, roll up the ends in the same manner as a cake roll. Make sure that you keep it tight and even. Wrap the roll in the parchment paper, seam side down, and place back in the freezer until firm—about 1 hour.

Slice cookies ¼-inch thick and place on cookie sheet at least 1 inch apart. Sprinkle brown sugar on the tops of cookies. Bake for 8–10 minutes until the edges just turn brown.

SCORE TIP:

LACTOSE-FREE PUMPKIN STRUDEL COOKIES

There are many choices when it comes to dairy-free butters. I use Earth Balance and have loved this product. It's great to bake with both savory and sweet items. The consistency and taste is exactly like real butter.

pomegranate-vanilla, blueberry-lemonade, and tangerine sorbets

POMEGRANATE-VANILLA SORBET

2½ cups water

2½ cups sugar

2 cups pomegranate juice

¼ cup tonic water

2 limes, squeezed

1 teaspoon of vanilla extract

EQUIPMENT:

sorbet/ice cream maker

Place water and sugar in saucepan and allow sugar to dissolve on medium heat. Add pomegranate juice, tonic, lime juice, and vanilla. Bring to boil and leave at rolling boil for 5–6 minutes. Take off heat and cool in fridge or ice water bath. When mixture is completely cooled, put in sorbet maker and make according to manufacturer's suggested directions. Place in freezer for several hours before serving.

BLUEBERRY-LEMONADE SORBET

2 cups water

2 cups sugar

½ cup lemon juice

1 cup blueberry juice

½ cup pureed blueberries

1 tablespoon lemon zest

EQUIPMENT:

sorbet/ice cream maker

In saucepan, add water and sugar. Dissolve sugar on medium heat. Add remainder of ingredients. Bring to boil and leave at rolling boil for 3–4 minutes. Take off heat and allow to cool in fridge or ice water bath. When mixture is completely chilled, put in sorbet maker and make according to manufacturer's suggested directions. Put in freezer for several hours before serving.

TANGERINE SORBET

2 cups water

2 cups sugar

2 cups fresh tangerine juice

½ cup orange juice

1 tablespoon lemon juice

EQUIPMENT:

sorbet/ice cream maker

In saucepan, add water and sugar. Dissolve sugar on medium heat. Add remainder of ingredients. Bring to boil and leave at rolling boil for 3–4 minutes. Take off heat and allow to cool in fridge or ice water bath. When mixture is completely chilled, put in sorbet maker and make according to manufacturer's suggested directions. Put in freezer for several hours before serving.

SCORE TIP:

POMEGRANATE-VANILLA, BLUEBERRY-LEMONADE, AND TANGERINE SORBETS

The options are endless when it comes to sorbet flavors. But do you know the difference between sorbets and sherbets? Sorbets are made with pureed fruits, sugar, and water. Sherbets are made with those three same ingredients, but they also contain milk, gelatin, or egg whites. The vast majority of sherbets, though, have some sort of milk or cream. A lot of individuals who really want ice cream but are not looking for all the fat and calories, might opt for sherbet. The added cream/milk ingredients in sherbet give that familiar texture of ice cream but reduce all the calories and fat. Sorbet on the other hand is great for individuals who are intolerant of or allergic to dairy. Also, if you're looking to reduce your sugar intake, have sherbet.

NOTE: if you cannot find tangerines in your local market, you can replace them with oranges. But no cheating and using processed orange juice. You will taste the difference by squeezing the oranges yourself. And think about it this way, you will get a great arm workout.

apple bourbon bread pudding with cinnamon ice cream

APPLE BOURBON BREAD PUDDING WITH CINNAMON ICE CREAM

YIELD: 4–6 SERVINGS

¾ stick butter

¾ cup dark brown sugar

⅓ cup sugar

2 apples (Pink Lady variety), cut up in small pieces

1 teaspoon cinnamon

¼ teaspoon nutmeg

pinch salt

⅓ cup bourbon

1 small baguette, cut in bite-sized pieces

2 cups crusty multigrain bread, cut in bite-sized pieces

2½ cups whole milk

4 eggs

½ cup Coffee Mate French vanilla

½ cup sugar

1 teaspoon vanilla extract

½ teaspoon cinnamon

cinnamon ice cream

Melt butter in a saucepan on medium heat. Add both sugars and incorporate. Add apples and mix together until apples are coated. Add bourbon, a little bit at a time. Let mixture cook down until all bourbon is dissolved. Cook for 20–22 minutes on medium-low heat until apples are soft.

Cut bread into small pieces and put in large bowl. In another bowl, mix milk, eggs, Coffee Mate, cinnamon, sugar, and vanilla. Whisk together until blended. Pour mixture over bread and incorporate. Let mixture sit for 20 minutes in fridge.

Line a large glass dish and set medium-sized ramekin cups inside. Put 2 tablespoons of apple mixture on the bottom of the ramekins. For large ramekins, add 3 tablespoons apple mixture. Add bread mixture until it reaches top of ramekin. Top again with 1 tablespoon apple mixture. Fill baking dish with hot water until water comes halfway up ramekin. Bake for 35–40 minutes at 375 degrees. Serve with cinnamon ice cream.

SCORE TIP:

APPLE BOURBON BREAD PUDDING WITH CINNAMON ICE CREAM

It is common today to find gourmet flavors of ice cream at your local food market. From Madagascar vanilla and salted caramel to pomegranate, there are many unique flavors on the market. You should be able to find cinnamon ice cream at your local market, but in case you can't, here's a substitute option. Put 4 scoops of vanilla ice cream into a bowl. Sprinkle 1 teaspoon of ground cinnamon on top. Mix together until all cinnamon is incorporated. Put back into freezer to harden. Voilà! Cinnamon ice cream.

french toast bread pudding with maple-walnut ice cream

FRENCH TOAST BREAD PUDDING WITH MAPLE-WALNUT ICE CREAM

YIELD: 4–6 SERVINGS

4 eggs

2½ cups whole milk

1 cup vanilla yogurt

⅓ cup real maple syrup

1 teaspoon vanilla

⅓ cup sugar

¼ teaspoon nutmeg

1 teaspoon cinnamon

¼ teaspoon all spice

12-14 slices cinnamon bread

½ cup raisins

½ cup pecans, chopped

½ teaspoon cinnamon

¼ teaspoon nutmeg

⅓ cup brown sugar

¼ cup butter, melted

Preheat oven to 375 degrees.

In medium bowl, mix eggs, milk, yogurt, maple syrup, vanilla, sugar, and spices. Whisk together until smooth and sugar is dissolved.

Lay bread slices on bottom of greased, medium-sized, glass baking dish. Leave no spaces. Pour a little mixture over the bread. Sprinkle 2–3 tablespoons raisins over bread and batter. Put another layer of bread slices on top, add batter and raisins.

Repeat until batter, bread, and raisins are gone.

In small bowl, mix cinnamon, nutmeg, pecans, brown sugar, and melted butter. Sprinkle on top of bread pudding mixture.

Cover dish with foil. Bake for 40–45 minutes. Remove foil after 25 minutes. Bake until golden brown and custard comes together. Serve with maple-walnut ice cream.

MAPLE-WALNUT ICE CREAM

1 cup real maple syrup

1½ cups heavy cream

½ cup whipping cream

1 cup whole milk

¼ teaspoon salt

2 large eggs

⅓ cup walnuts, toasted and chopped

EQUIPMENT:

ice cream maker

Boil syrup in a heavy saucepan over moderately high heat. Stir in creams, milk, and salt and bring to a boil over moderate heat.

Whisk eggs in large bowl and then add hot cream mixture in a slow stream while whisking. Transfer to saucepan and cook over moderately low heat, stirring constantly until slightly thickened. Do not boil.

Cool mixture for at least 3 hours.

Make ice cream according to manufacturer's directions. Once ice cream comes together in ice-cream maker, add walnuts. Continue churning ice cream until frozen, then transfer to an airtight container and put in freezer to harden.

CONCLUSION

As you read the stories from my past, you can see the special a bond with food that has infiltrated my life. I was destined to become a chef and all the events that have taken place over the course of my life have led me to where I am today.

I wrote this book when living in the Northeast. Since then my life has changed for the better. It was a tough road that I endured and I became a stronger person from all my experiences—especially with the help of all the individuals I mentioned in my stories. When I changed my life to pursue my dreams and passion, I had no idea what the outcome would be, but I went for it. There was no looking back. I'm glad I had love and support behind me because otherwise I would have given up a long time ago. That's why food and people go hand and hand—not because we need food to nourish ourselves every day but because of that special bond between humans and food that creates long-lasting memories. Just think about all the happy moments in your life. Were you alone? No, you were probably with friends, family, and the people who mattered most in your life. And you may have had some crazy experiences like mine, but they will be memorable. I know I have many more memorable experiences coming up, and my journey continues. So stay tuned. It's about to get exciting!

Outtakes

Jenn-ism Glossary

FSSU (Fuck Some Shit Up) - say this when you want to kick some ass at something. When this exact phrase is said, you will FSSU!

Example: *"So, Jenn, are you ready for your half marathon tomorrow?"*

"Yeah! I'm going to FSSU and kick some ass!"

What, what – recite with a little hand gesture. "Raise the roof" with both hands a slight lean back with your shoulders saying, "What, what!" This can be said on any occasion and at any time.

Example: *"Look at what I just did. I made some yummy bacon powder. What, what!"*

Get an F'n job – a phrase I say quite a lot for people that chose not to work, that are very cable of working but choose to milk the system.

Word up – a term used to greet someone that is your friend, who is hip and cool.

Example: *"Hey, homes, word up!"*

Be right back, doll – a phrase to use in Vegas when you're talking to the concierge trying to figure out what to do for the night, you're hung-over, heat exhausted from lying in the sun all day, stuffed from eating too much, and haggard from an unnecessary run on the tread mill. After saying, "Be right back, doll," you proceed to lie on the floor because you can't stand up any longer.

I ain't mad at ya – a term of endearment when telling someone that you're not angry with them.

We're looking good and feeling good – a term you can use on any occasion to make yourself or a group of people feel good. Use as a self-affirmation.

Example: *Running a race and you're at mile 20; "Hey, Dave. I feel wrecked and can't feel my legs, but I'm still looking good and feeling good. Now where is that damn finish line?"*

And we're walking, and we're breathing - say this phrase slowly and quietly to calm yourself and find your inner peace. This is said usually when you're nervous about something, about to give a big presentation to a large group of people, or do something that you've never done before. Using this mantra can help you feel calm in any situation.

Example: *"I need to calm myself down before I give this big presentation to the board of directors. And we're walking and we're breathing…and we're calming."*

Aaand were back – a multipurpose saying that can be used several ways. Use when calling a person back after a call is dropped. Use this phrase if someone you're with gets lost in the moment or goes into a dreamlike state then comes out of it.

Sip, sip, stir, stir – an action that occurs when you're cooking and drinking in your kitchen, all at the same time. Best results occur when you repeat several times!

Wee - a phrase my friend, Megan, and I used repeatedly on the beautiful islands of Hawaii. Use this to show excitement and happiness in situations where you're about to do something exhilarating or you're just plain happy.

Example: *"I can't believe we're about to go snorkeling for the first time. Hope we don't see any sharks out here. Wee!"*

High kicks – this saying/gesture can be used in any situation. The phrase is normally followed by a high kick with either leg. These words are used when you're excited about something or something exciting just happened to you.

That is not the correct nomenclature – a term that my friend Scott Schoneman said while my friend Alisa and I were in NYC. Though the word means to choose names for things, especially in a science discipline we took this term and used it however we wanted and in any context. It makes you look smart, rich, and cultured.

Example: *"Hey, Scott! That was an incredible brunch-place you took Alisa and I too; you have really nomenclatured yourself today!" or, "Wow! That cab ride was straight-up nomenclature!"*

I'm wrecked – a term used when you're completely exhausted, worn-out, or spent and feel like you were run over by a semi-truck.